TIME TO GO

TIME TO GO

Guy Kennaway

MENSCH PUBLISHING

Mensch Publishing
51 Northchurch Road, London N1 4EE, United Kingdom

First published in Great Britain 2019

A catalogue record for this book is available from the British Library

ISBN: HB: 978-1-912914-00-5; EBOOK: 978-1-912914-01-2;
EPDF: 978-1-912914-02-9

2 4 6 8 10 9 7 5 3 1

Typeset by Newgen KnowledgeWorks Pvt. Ltd., Chennai, India
Printed and bound in Great Britain by CPI Group (UK) Ltd, Croydon CR0 4YY

It is often said it is better to leave too early rather than too late …
whether it be a job, a party or life itself.

Henry Marsh

In memoriam S. 1927–2018

CONTENTS

CONTENTS

ACKNOWLEDGEMENTS

Quite a few people helped me get this book from my mind to the shelf, and I would like to thank them.

First is Jay Jopling, whose incisive mind and ringing laughter have left their mark on every page.

Stan Stanton, my friend and agent, whose opinion is always spot on, encouraged me every step of the way.

Richard Charkin, my friend and publisher, made the ride so enjoyable.

Thank you also to Peter Gill for giving the text a fine polish.

Love and gratitude also goes in abundance to Paul Fryer, my dialogue coach, joke barometer, and much much more.

My sister Emma kept me writing through many doubt-laden days. Her skill, determination and undimmable spirit are a constant inspiration.

Thank you to my book club: Fiona, Bundle, John, Tessa, Louise, Maymie, Catherine, Tamsin, Nellie and Caroline, whose love of literature, or at least books, and the conversations about them, made me want to supply them with a good read and a lively discussion.

My creative writing group here in Pilton were also helpful in a more technical way. Thank you James, Vicki, Katherine and Brigid.

I thank also Amanda Chambers, for her kindness, and Haruka, Paul, Paula and their kids for their hospitality. And of course my thanks go to Nanna.

If readers are interested in the subjects in this book, I recommend looking at *Being Mortal* by Atul Gawande and anything written by Henry Marsh.

If you want to hear me talking about this book and some of the other things that crop up between birth and death, download the weekly podcast I do with Paul Fryer, called *That's Just Ridiculous with Guy & Paul.*

Finally, I must thank my mother, Susie Kennaway, for being a brilliant subject, a great sport and an all-round tour de force.

ONE

The first pressing

I WAS BATTLING THROUGH A swift visit to my elderly mother in France when she took me aside and told me she had something important she wanted to ask me, but it was *privée*. She was not French, but had lived there for thirty years, and liked to sprinkle a few French words around to set her, if not above, then at least apart from the expatriates who had not properly learnt to speak the language.

Susie moved to the Tarn, a region slap in the middle of France just above the Pyrenees, with her third husband Stanley, in their prime, thirty years before. She had been 50, and he 60, and both were beautiful, talented, bold and sexy, and both threw themselves into creating an enviable home in an expansive garden, which rang with conversation and laughter.

But time was a cruel companion. And it was particularly unforgiving when you spent long days in its company sunbathing, gardening, drinking and eating rich food. By 2017 Stanley and Susie were old and bent, with thinning hair and sun-beaten skin.

One thing that always brought a sparkle to Susie's pale blue rheumy eyes was a secret, whether it was sharing one or prising one out of someone, and I could see her excitement as she crept towards her bedroom, and her impatience at finding Stanley blocking the door with his walking frame. On its ledge was a tube of ointment.

I loudly said 'Got your KY jelly Stan!'

Without missing a beat he croaked 'I'm afraid there's no call for that these days.' But at dinner the night before I had seen him pat my girlfriend Amanda's bottom as she passed him with the dishes. He had been pulling his *Rodin prepares to enter the disrobing room* face.

Susie shut the door and directed me to a chair that looked as if it was in a prearranged spot. She liked to arrange things carefully, and aimed to leave nothing to chance. As she sat agonisingly slowly in front of me, the little explosions of pain from her crumbling and twisted vertebrae almost audible, I wondered what this was about. Secrets usually meant trouble with Susie. In our family, if you wanted to keep something quiet, Mum was most definitely not the word. And she was never usually interested in my opinion, or indeed anyone's for that matter, unless it was an accurate reproduction of her own. I braced myself for trouble, as things were never straightforward with her. A request for a favour or the offer of a gift was usually part of some stratagem that only she knew the full extent of and which – when fully revealed – turned out to be a nasty surprise.

This account might be easier to read, though not tell, if Susie were a kindly, pinafore-wearing, apple-cheeked granny who lived only to show baskets of kittens to indulged grandchildren. But she was much better than that. She was a real person, who a long and varied life had knocked about a fair bit, leaving chunks missing from her personality and scar tissue from emotional wounds that still howled in pain many decades later. She was certainly no Mrs Tiggywinkle, and I would not patronise her by softening her edges and sweetening her behaviour the way elderly people so often are in literature and on film. Susie was a woman of passion, anger and determination. She still relished revenge and had many scores to settle. If anything, old age had sharpened, not mellowed, her.

'I have had a wonderful life,' she said to me, holding her hand in front of her mouth I feared because she was self-conscious about her teeth. 'I have lived in beautiful houses, and here we had the garden, which has been such an enormous success. Did I tell you that the mayor asked me to enter it into a competition for the best floral village in the south of France? I won a puce cyclamen,' she both sneered and preened. 'He's such a nice man, and cultured, not like an English mayor, you know, common, quite, quite different. Of course I lived in London and America in the 60s with your father, and Gloucestershire after that, before it was ruined, and had the restaurant and the film company and so many happy times …' Her eyes were glistening as her memory reeled back a heavily edited version of her life. A competitive element had entered the discourse, as it so often did with her. She wanted to remind me that her life had not only been good, but the best. 'I have met so many interesting people. Well, your father and I knew the best of the film and literary world. And people were much more interesting than they are now. You wouldn't have any idea of how much better life was before your generation. But I know you know that. And Stanley and I have been on so many amazing holidays, been to China, and India …'

She was indeed a member of the generation and class that had tasted the first pressing of the olive oil of modern life. Its members had enjoyed speedy promotion in interesting jobs, spacious houses, meaningful holidays, cars to drive on empty roads and cheap fuel to put in their tanks, and it was now her grandchildren's generation that was left to live off the congealed chip fat that remained.

She shook her head. 'After a life like mine, I don't want to have to live in a care home. No, Guy, I will not be put in a home. I will not be.'

I certainly sympathised with that. I wouldn't like to live with my life reduced to a couple of framed photos, a wingback chair and a small TV. I had sympathies also for the hapless patients cooped up with Susie who would have to live out their last days listening to how glamorous and eventful her life had been compared to their tiny, fruitless existence.

'So *j'aidecidé* that I shall end my life, here, in this wonderful house, with Stanley.'

'OK,' I said. 'What do you mean exactly?'

'We have decided to, er, kill ourselves,' she smiled, 'on the same day, at the same time. I want to go out at the top. At a time of our choosing. But I have one little problem, which is why I am asking for your help. I need to get hold of the right drugs to do it. Can you buy me some heroin?'

I leant back in my chair and tried to gather my thoughts. It perturbed me to think of her contemplating death. I had always thought that she would go on forever, pickled as she was in defiance, revenge and resentment. I was Prince Charles to her Queen, destined never to take my place at the head of the family (though I somewhat doubted Her Majesty was asking Charles to score her smack). But with our parents racing through their 80s, my generation had turned into eternal children. And my mother emanated, even in her recent diminished and bent form, so much power.

When I spoke, I told Susie that I was shocked.

She barely listened. 'Can you get hold of some for me?' she asked.

'Well ... I might be able to track *some* down ... but, aren't you allergic to morphine?'

'Yes,' she said.

'Heroin is from the same family as morphine, from the opium poppy ...' As I spoke, I thought about that family, the one with heroin and morphine in it. Perhaps the only family I knew of as strange as ours.

'Ah. Then we shall have to go another route,' she said. 'But what do you suggest?' She leant forward. 'Will you help me?'

'What about Switzerland?' I asked.

'It's no good,' she waved her hand impatiently. 'You need a certificate signed by two doctors, which means you basically have to have a terminal illness.'

Sounded like classic Swiss thoroughness.

'Do you remember us taking you skiing as a child?'

'Yes,' I said.

'Of course your father and I lived through the golden era of skiing. Empty runs, just a few English people. And the *right* sort. The only pity was that we had to take you. It was never as good again after that. Everyone was so nice, so interesting. Not like now.'

TWO

Pernod, sunshine and siestas

SUNDAY EVENING IN THE Ryanair shed of Toulouse Airport, eating my third panini, and staring at the passengers in the speedy boarding queue, I was reminded how mummy dressed for air travel.

But first I think we need to talk about nomenclature. *Mummy*. There are difficulties with this. It's how I address her, and how I usually refer to her behind her back, but on the page the word pongs of privilege, with a top note of Norman Bates. Since turning sixty I had found it increasingly hard to say *Mummy*, particularly in public. It was a symptom of the Prince Charles eternal son syndrome. My strategy was to mumble the word, because the woman baulked at *mum*. My sisters Emma and Jane had both transitioned to *mother*, though Jane threw in a few *mumsies* to keep it casual. I couldn't see that as a solution. Calling her *Mummy* made me sound weird, calling her *mother* made her sound weird.

I am going to use *mum*, not to annoy her, though I think it will, but because it seems simplest, and I will add *Susie* for variation.

When flying, Susie favoured an ensemble with an ambitious touch, like a linen suit and hat, and often a new pair of shoes that pinched her feet. But she refused to use a wheelchair, and only recently had accepted a ride on those beeping golf carts. The bar for disability at airports was set low. I often smiled at what thirty years ago would have been considered a miracle, but now was an unremarkable event: someone standing up from a wheelchair.

My mum had known the glory years of international air travel, between the first transatlantic flight and the birth of Ryanair. Or was it 9/11 that did for it, with the glamour-sapping security measures it forced on us all? My father took full advantage of the new freedoms of the age of Aquarius, and he and my mum, sometimes with me and my siblings, jetted around the world and lived in many beautiful places: Allassio, Kashmir, Malibu, and Minorca, when the Balearics really were sleepy deserted islands long before mass tourism. We lived in a farmhouse a short walk from a deserted beach through an olive grove ringing with crickets. We never saw a tourist. There were none in those days. We four children grew up suntanned with no fear of cancer, and ran free in the era before paedophiles and road traffic shut down childhood. My parents seemed to have had an equally good time. They, after all, had discovered in about three years, wine, garlic, olive oil, Pernod, sunshine and siestas.

Susie *had* had a good life. But even so, something in her plan didn't quite add up for me.

The principal flaw was that she wasn't ill or that infirm. I have friends who after an agonised discussion with siblings and doctors have reluctantly agreed to put a Do Not Resuscitate Order on a parent or grandparent. But these oldies were in tumorous pain, incontinent, and/or lost to this world, incapable of remembering their own or their children's names. Their lives were as hopeless as a dried out hanging basket.

My mum could get up, dress herself, call friends, go shopping, write emails, cook lunch, track down the mayor and issue a bollocking in French about some minor village issue, lie on the sofa with *The Guardian* digest, rise at six, pour three or four whiskies without spilling a drop, cook a three-course meal, and settle back on the sofa to follow the complex plot of a box set before undressing, removing her make-up and reading a decent book prior to an undisturbed night of sleep.

On this most recent visit she had told me she was landscaping the village car park and planning to write a new book. The landscaping project was the consequence of her having persuaded the Commune to chop down two ancient plane trees that were partially obscuring the view from her sitting room. With plant catalogues open on her desk, she was throwing herself into the task of proving to the Commune how superior a plants' woman she was.

When last year she had started complaining about the trees in her view, everyone who knew her said 'Susie, forget the trees, the view is still beautiful, and for half the year they won't have any leaves on them.'

The view was indeed majestic even with the trees standing. From Susie's grey cotton sofas you could see for twenty-five miles across a classic French pastoral quilt of fields, stone farmsteads, oak woods and cute villages – each with a steeple. The trees in the foreground were about forty yards from the house, and obscured a *small* portion of the vista. They were a minor irritant, best ignored. Any attempt to remove them would frustrate her, annoy her neighbours, turn the mayor against her, and make things worse – we all said. This was discussed against the background of two obsessive court cases she had pursued for years against neighbours for things they did that annoyed her. Dismissing our advice, she lobbied and she cajoled and sure enough, she got them cut down. This was not the act of a geriatric letting the reins of life fall from feeble hands. It was the machinations of a determined and effective woman enjoying her power. So why had she asked me about killing herself?

I also remembered that on the second day of my four-day visit Susie had instructed me to pick up some heavy box files and take them through to the kitchen. She kept huge amounts of old papers, in files, in plastic boxes and in steel cabinets that were always close to hand. She stood behind me, a small, twisted woman with knobbly knuckles, watching everything I did as if she didn't have enough faith in me to carry a plastic box from one room to another without messing up.

'Move that one, push it forwards, that's it,' she instructed, just before I was about to do precisely that. 'Put it over there,' she pointed at the kitchen table – the only feasible surface to put it on. I turned to get the second box as she said 'Now get the other one.'

In one box was the transcript of the Appeal Court Case Susie was involved in during the 1980s against a neighbour who was making an ugly noise powerboating on a lake a quarter of a mile from her house. The case is called Kennaway vs Thomson & Another, for those of you insane enough to want to look it up. She won. She always did. It established the principle that moving to a nuisance does not mitigate the nuisance. Susie was basically responsible for developers being able to erect blocks of yuppy flats in the middle of cities and close down live music venues, even though they had been entertaining locals for years.

'I'm going to write a book about the powerboat case,' she told me. 'I've read the court transcripts. They are absolutely riveting. Do take a look.'

She was embarking on a book, at 87 years of age. It seemed an unusual thing to do while actively planning suicide, though it is an activity that drives many writers to think about doing themselves in.

She delved into the second box. 'Here are the contracts for *Silence*.'

Silence was a novel that my father, James Kennaway, was writing when he was killed in a car crash aged 40 in 1968. A Welshman called Lynn finished it, piecing together the various drafts. I heard, though I do not know if it is true, that when James died they found in the top pocket of his suit jacket a bit of paper with the last sentence of *Silence* written on it, a sentence that unfortunately I do not have to hand. It's something about the girl being led away to an awful noise. Susie had received some enquiries about the movie rights, possibly because – in Trump's new America – the novel's themes of race, violence, guilt and redemption now struck a chord in film-makers. She fiddled about in the box and withdrew an old shiny photocopied document. She wanted to know if the TV rights belonged to her.

I leafed through the contract, dated 1973, which was 45 pages long, and started reading it. Within seconds my mind numbed. This was work for a keen young lawyer, not me. I did notice on the very first page it said she was paid $100,000 in 1973, a sum so large it was hard to believe she hadn't sold all the broadcast rights in perpetuity. I decided that nothing good was going to come from this, but said nothing. I sighed and stopped reading. Susie meanwhile dragged a chair ten inches across the floor, sat down and commenced reading the numbered paragraphs.

After twenty minutes she said 'Look at this,' and slid page 15 to me. I read it. It seemed to indicate that the rights to the movie reverted to my dad (and therefore her), if the movie were not made within twenty years of the signing of the contract. No movie of *Silence* had ever been made.

'You see,' she said. 'It's always worth checking the small print.'

We asked Stanley, who was a showbiz accountant before he retired, to look at the contract, and after taking about a quarter of an hour to manoeuvre – with his Scotch – to the table, he too sat down and read page 1 and page 15 before saying, 'There seems to be a contradiction here.' Then he lost the thread, and said 'I remember when Franco was making *Taming of The Shrew* and I went down onto the set and accidentally walked into the girls' changing room and they were all entirely naked but none of them minded as I was just the accountant. Quite amazing really how they carried on, just walking past me without a stitch on, breasts on full display ...' he disappeared into the reverie. Susie gave him a sharp look, then drilled back into the detail of the contract.

I had meanwhile found a letter in the file from Lynn Hughes, the guy who finished *Silence* after James died. He complained that he was to receive no money for any of the film rights. Susie had clearly nixed that. He was never mentioned by her except when absolutely necessary, and then usually as 'that odd Welshman.' I have often wondered how much work he did on the novel. His contribution was wiped clean in her version, the official version, of events. She had a habit of silencing or ridiculing people who didn't agree with her reality. But it was immensely impressive that this bent old lady in her ninth decade had read through a complex contract and found what could be an important clause that no one else had noticed. She was by no means an aged woman in steep mental decline. So why had she started thinking of bowing out of a life that looked pretty full from where I was standing (or, rather, slouching in an airport chair)?

One theory I was considering was that she was running out of money, and too proud to face poverty in old age. That could explain her looking at the contract again. Maybe a large payment for an option on an American mini-series of *Silence* would push the death operation onto the back burner?

The departure gate opened. I stayed put while I watched the English passengers, many of whom looked like people not on holiday but on a visit to either their own second home or, like me, a family member's. Another idea crossed my mind. Susie always liked to make a public statement, and take a political stand. I wondered whether politics was behind her request for the poison? The United Kingdom had just voted to leave the EU, and she, like hundreds of thousands of UK citizens who had feathered comfortable nests in European sunshine, felt angry and rejected by both the Brits, and recently the French (though actually Susie made a point of saying how mortified all her French friends were about the result). If she and Stanley killed themselves simultaneously it would surely be a news item, particularly if it coincided with a letter from her to *The Times* or *Figaro* or wherever she wrote her letters these days, and I could imagine the headline: THE HUMAN COST OF BREXIT. She would become a martyr, and a liberal one at that. I could see that appealing to her. She was the kind of woman who wanted noble things said about her after her death. *She died for a cause she believed in,* would be an epitaph that appealed to her.

I watched the passengers pushing to get onto the plane. Why? The interior of a Ryanair aircraft was the only place I could think of uglier and less comfortable than the Ryanair departure shed; why intensify the agony? And another thought crossed my mind: if she did pull off her plan, and the newspapers made a thing of it, the Gendarmes might also take an interest, and investigate these unusual deaths, specifically to see whether anyone had aided and abetted their demise, and who knows, through Interpol, after discovering I was the last to be with them, they might requisition my laptop and take a trip back through its incriminating search history. And what was the one thing Susie had made me promise before leaving? To

Google "quick and painless non-opiate poisons". So that was her game: to get the publicity she so loved for her political views and see me banged up in a hellhole Marseille gaol doing a twelve-year stretch for murder. A win–win.

THREE

We could have got an eight-ball

A COUPLE OF MONTHS LATER, in mid-December, we had clarified that the TV rights to *Silence* had already been sold, and the UK Government were heading for a Brexit that could well leave expatriates out in the cold. Susie feared that she would be sent back to the UK, which after years of insulting the place, would be hard for her to pull off with any aplomb. Backing down wasn't her thing. I had told her that a mass expulsion scenario seemed unlikely. But even if she were allowed to remain in France, she was faced with a second doomsday: withdrawal of free access to the French health service. She, like many expatriates in the Tarn to whom I had spoken, had often boasted about how good the French service was compared to the NHS, and she had long ago cancelled her Bupa subscription, and there was no chance at her age with her arthritis and heart problems that Bupa would open its arms to her again. After years of leisurely good-natured house visits by the local French doctor and short-notice appointments with hospital consultants in Toulouse, Susie was staring down the barrel of underfunded British

NHS treatment with its blockaded A&E departments, harassed GPs and six-month waits for a specialist.

I rang Susie to see how she was.

She said 'I'm not taking Stanley shopping again – ever. He collapsed in the Leclerc car park, and couldn't get up. Luckily some people ran to help him. The *only* thing in his trolley was bottles. It was so embarrassing.'

She had bought him a travel wheelchair. It weighed 5 kg. 'I can't lift it, but he can. So I push it to the car and Stanley puts it in. I am taking it out with me, not to be wheeled around in it ...' She couldn't take that. Her pride wouldn't let her. 'I take it to the garden centre, and put things in it, and use it to rest.' She has allowed herself to use it as long as no one is pushing it.

There was no talk of murder.

But when I rang her just before Christmas she started the conversation with one word: 'Cocaine.'

'What do you mean?'

'Cocaine, as a means of dying.' She had lowered her voice, not that she needed to if it were Stanley in the house. You could shout *I am going to kill us both*! and he would smile amiably and say 'Oh. Is it nearly drinks time? Jolly good.'

'An overdose,' Susie continued. 'I have a friend here who mentioned it.' The friend was an old lady Susie had recently met. She got close to people quickly, and then usually bust up with them a few years later. Who knew what their crime was? Sometimes it emerged only decades after. One exile had called her cucumber soup salty. Others were banished for a lesser offence. I have seen many people travel this arc with her. Almost everyone she was rude about – and there were many – she had once adored. They all crossed her in one way or another and there was never any going back with her.

This meant she had to be good at finding someone to fill the gaps so often created in her group of friends, and she had become adept at that. All my life people have told me how wonderful and brilliant my mum is, though many I never saw again. I can think of three or four straight away, and I don't know what they did to have disappeared, but perhaps they are lucky to have got away. Resentments energised her. They lit up her eyes and drew her mouth into a little private smile as she momentarily thought about how best to act on them.

'She is ninety-one and bright as a button,' Susie told me on the phone, adding, 'we agree about everything.' They wouldn't have been friends if she hadn't agreed with everything Susie said. She was the one who had suggested cocaine, which meant that Susie must have brought the subject up. I had wondered whether she was polishing the plan by running it past a few people.

I mentioned to her that cocaine might not create the effect she desired, and perk her up rather than send her off. I said most people only died of cocaine after about twenty years of miserable misuse.

'It's not the right way,' I said.

'Well I'm relying on you,' she said.

I wasn't comfortable being relied on to kill someone, even her, who I must admit I had had murderous thoughts about. I put the phone down and thought about Susie and Stanley wired on coke: the house a complete tip; the curtains closed at 4 p.m.; Stanley on the phone trying to hurry up the dealer; my mum searching through the garbage in case she had chucked out a wrap with some grains in it; the two of them bickering.

'If you hadn't spent so much on the garden furniture, we could have got had an eight-ball. But oh no, you had to have your wicker-effect coffee table with toughened glass top.' Stanley, in my scenario, says.

'I saw you doing an extra line on it!' Susie snaps back.

'I didn't.' says Stanley.

'You did. Don't deny it! I'm looking after it this time. I can't trust you.' My mum pours the garbage across the trellised terrace she was once so proud of and, with creaking joints and heavy breathing, gets down on her hands and knees to comb through it.

'You'll only lose it,' Stanley mouths to himself.

'We better get this place cleared up before the kids come for the weekend.' Susie says. 'Help me up.'

Into the phone Stanley hisses 'Shit. Answer, won't you?'

I went to dinner at my friends Paul and Elinor's house the following week. They lived in a mammoth glass-walled studio overlooking the Thames Barrier. The dinner was served at a long table under a parachute draped from the ceiling to keep the guests warm. I was sitting next to my Swedish friend Vanessa, whose father had inexplicably committed suicide with a gun when he was in his forties, and I wanted her advice on my predicament.

I described how Susie planned to choose the time and place of not just her death but Stanley's too. It was to be in their bedroom, a double suicide, geriatric, but with a hint of Romeo and Juliet. Susie was going to be in control right to the very end. I told Vanessa that my mum had asked me to find the poison to send them off.

I imparted my latest theory: Susie was going to double-cross Stanley in the final moment, to get his money – what little there was left of it – and, more importantly, to get one final thing over on him: the last word. She liked to have that. I described to Vanessa the picture I had in my mind of my mother and Stanley sitting on the edge of the well-made bed, in the scrupulously tidy bedroom (explaining that Susie would be wanting to make a good impression even after she died), each holding a pill in their hands.

She would be in charge, and say 'OK, on three. One, two, three,' and Stan would pop the pill in his mouth and open his eyes in childish wonder, the way he did when he did something silly (which was quite often), and Susie would just pretend to put the pill in her mouth, so she could then watch him keel over and die on the bed while she threw her pill out of the window into the spring sunshine and get on with her day. I had this idea that she was going to pick a sunny spring day, as she would want everything to look as lovely as possible. After checking he was a goner, she would go downstairs and start ringing everyone with the news. She always liked to break bad news.

Vanessa listened and then burst out laughing. 'Oh but Guy. Don't you see?' she said. 'It is *you* your mother is going to kill, not your stepfather. Just as you say you have wanted in the past to kill her, so now she wants to kill *you*. Of course she knows what you have been thinking. Call it a mother's instinct. So you bring her the poison and she says, before you go, I just want a last cup of tea with my son … and then she stirs the shit into *your* mug.' Vannessa laughed again. 'Be very careful Guy. Poison is not discriminating. I hope you have an antidote, man.'

I thought about this. Susie liked to get even, it was true. The matter was never closed with her. But banishment, not murder, was her main tool. Although … maybe she was stepping up the ante? And it wouldn't surprise me if she *did* want to kill me. Almost everyone else did, at some point or another. Mostly for perfectly understandable reasons.

My relationship with Susie has had its ups and downs over the years, and it is fair to say that advancing age, maturity and mellowness have not entirely smoothed our troubles away.

The principal charge laid against me in the bustling court of Susie's mind, was that I had failed to be the right person. I wasn't sufficiently the son she had ordered. From time to time, for instance, I disagreed, or as she saw it, treacherously took the wrong side against her. And she didn't forget a slight. She not so much harboured grudges, as dry-docked them for a full refit, so they were seaworthy whenever she needed to relaunch them. At 78, she could still remember being placed in the wrong seat at a lunch party in 1968, along with about 900 other perceived slights in the intervening years. She was pickled in resentments, though it had a deceptively sweet taste to those who don't know the ingredients.

FOUR

The man by the lake

THIS WASN'T THE FIRST time that assisted suicide had arisen with my mum. In the late 1960s Susie had given Beryl, my grandfather's perky secretary and girlfriend, a help out of life. She had told me the story many times. Beryl had had cancer. James, my father, was in America. 'Probably with another woman,' Susie said the last time she talked about Beryl. An interesting detail, and inevitably correct. He was off being an adulterer, leaving his wife at home to become a murderer. Beryl was in the final agonising tussle with the tumour and going to die anyway, I should point out, and as Susie often said, recently with an edge of envy, 'things were so different then, you could just do it without anyone asking any questions ...'

Before my dad died in 1968, as I said, at just 40 years' old, Susie was quite a different woman. She had not developed into the indomitable Susie I knew in my adulthood. For a start she was staying at home while her husband swanned around here and there. I couldn't see Stanley being allowed to do that.

Despite, and possibly also because, Susie had grown so close to Beryl throughout her illness, at some point she and Doctor Gravesend (well named for this story) decided that Beryl had suffered enough. Susie told me what then happened. The doctor rigged up a morphine drip on a stepladder and attached it to Beryl's forearm. He then went downstairs and burnt all the drugs' packaging on the fire. Nice detail. There *were* legal issues even then. Susie bid him goodnight, saw him out, and returned upstairs to say goodbye to Beryl.

From the bedside Susie heard the doorbell ring, and when she answered it found Beryl's estranged mother standing there in the darkness. She had decided to make an unannounced visit, on the spur of the moment, to patch things up with her daughter. My mum must immediately have thought of the drip above Beryl's bed with the skull and cross-bones on it. I made that last bit up, but there would no doubt have been something about that stepladder that was difficult to explain because Susie said 'I'll just go and freshen her up,' rushed upstairs and took the drip out.

Beryl opened her eyes and said 'I was meeting an old man by the lake. I want to go back.'

My mum tried to hide the stepladder in the wardrobe but it wouldn't fit, so she opened the french window and took the ladder out onto the terrace and sneaked it bent double under the sitting-room window that Beryl's mum was quite possibly looking out of. Susie then crawled back to the bedroom, closed the patio doors and went to get Beryl's mum.

Beryl was still alive, but probably not in the best of shape. She saw her mother. I'm not sure if there was a rapprochement. At some point Beryl's mother left and Susie plugged the drip back in.

So Susie had form, or at least knew the gig. And Beryl went down to meet the old man by the lake.

FIVE

Turn-ups

T HE ARTIST PAUL FRYER came to stay with me in Somerset. With his raven black hair, dark eyes and compelling presence he always seemed to know what to do, even when it was the wrong thing. He dressed flamboyantly and had a penchant for costume. Over the past year he had turned up at my house garbed as a Bedouin, a Crusader, and a flirty housewife in a sensible frock. As an artist he was best known for his immense electrical devices. He liked to think big. He enjoyed science and knew a bit about chemistry. He manufactured his own drugs, and was always telling me about chemical compounds (though his DMT turned out to be useless to the point of legal when I smoked a pipe of it). He had arrived last summer for the Glastonbury Festival in a baggy white suit with his turn-ups full of pills. He picked out a handful and beamed a smile. 'The on button' he said. The pills in the other leg were the off button.

We went to eat at Gigi's, an old-school Italian restaurant in Glastonbury. It had an aquarium with a rubber fish, a faded poster of the Colosseum in very light traffic, and a framed photo of Sophia Loren on the Artex wall.

Paul warmed to the place and said it reminded him of Mama Mia in Leeds. These old-wave Italian and French restaurants were getting thinner on the ground, but were more authentic than many of the ones that were replacing them, like Frankie & Johnnies or Café Rouge. A middle-aged woman sat at the desk in the corner and totted up the bills. I must have been to Gigi's forty times in the past three years but because they had given up looking for repeat customers – all their trade apart from me was tourists – they always greeted me as a new-comer. When I paid, the woman always asked 'Where are you-a from?'

At dinner, I asked Paul to recommend a cocktail for mum. He said without hesitation

'Nitrogen. It's what the CIA use in political assassinations if they don't want any traces to be left.'

'How does it work? Isn't nitrogen relatively neutral?' I asked.

'Yes. That's how it works. Ordinary air is about 70 per cent nitrogen and 20 per cent oxygen. But we need that oxygen to live. So pure nitrogen gently deprives the body of oxygen. You don't even realise you are dying.'

It sounded quite promising. Almost relaxing.

'How does she take it?' I asked.

'Best done in a Spitfire gas mask,' Paul replied munching on battered calamari. 'I've got two.'

I imagined my mum lying on the bed with a fighter-pilot gas mark strapped to her face. It was not the image she was after. Not Ophelia on the bed, with Stanley as her Hamlet. (Stan was not ideally cast as Hamlet. He was a Pandarus at a push. He was not a man of introspection, except when he was wondering how near it was to drinks time and what a certain woman would look like naked.) And Ophelia was very wrong too. Let's be honest, it's Lady Macbeth, though I have no idea of the actual fantasy in Susie's head.

The deathbed image that she imagined would be photographed and published in newspapers (even in 2017 she considered the Internet irrelevant) was of her lying on a lacy bedspread, composed, resolute, like those marble effigies you see in churches. Not dead but asleep. Though in this case not asleep but dead. Thus she conquered even death. Her sunny bedroom filled with soft spring light. The clothes folded in the drawers. Her last to-do list fully completed. Dressing gowns hung up, shoes in pairs. The en suite bathroom sparkling. Stanley and her, laid side by side, holding hands, as though taking an after-lunch nap. Stanley, his eyes closed, but for once not snoring or dribbling. A few well-chosen books (for the photo, not for reading) on the bedside table. Downstairs everything was in order. Maybe a few glasses and a bottle of bubbly on the kitchen island for the pompiers who would tramp in with their heavy boots, and after being told by the doctor that there was no hope, retire respectfully downstairs, drink Susie's health and exchange stories about what a wonderful woman she was, and how brave to chose the place and time of her death. Some of them would have had previous dealings with her. She loved the pompiers. Her voice fluttered as she said the word. They were one of a number of subjects to which she frequently returned to prove the superiority of life in France over that in Britain. The doctor was another one. The district nurse a third. The mayor, as we know, another. Add the politeness of French children, and of course the food and drink, and she had quite enough to keep the theme alive for as long as you could listen.

The pompiers were a sign of how magnificent French men are. The implication being that the British are useless. They used to roar round in their fire engine to her place when she lived out in the country and crash through the front door in heavy boots and gauntlets to lift Stanley onto the bed when he fell over. Four of them. Without complaint. From Susie's telling, they seemed somehow to feel it was a privilege to spend an hour or two doing this. She would open a bottle of fizz for them afterwards, and flirt with them and entrance them with stories about her glamorous past while I imagine somewhere – on the other side of the Tarn – a house burnt down.

I couldn't see a British fireman putting up with her for long.

'You use pure nitrogen,' Paul continued. 'The brain doesn't panic. It doesn't notice, and British Oxygen, ironically, will deliver a cylinder. I've got the number. You have to put a deposit on the bottle but it's refundable.' Susie would like that thrifty touch. It might require a codicil to her will. She loved those. They were her chief disciplinary tool among her family. *To my first-born son Guy I leave the returned deposit on the nitrogen canister.*

We were discussing other options, Paul running through a list of nerve agents he was familiar with. 'The KGB love poison. They killed a man the other week in Istanbul.'

The waiter passing the table with a pizza, heard, stopped and said 'Si, with a poison umbrella.'

We turned to look at him. This felt like a major breach in security to me. Even the waiter in Gigi's knew what I was planning. But it was a good idea. You could kill Stanley with an umbrella very effectively. You'd just hand it to him and watch him trip over it and smash his head.

But the umbrella fatality did start me thinking along a different and possibly more fruitful line: political assassination. Of Susie, by a foreign power. My hands would be clean. In the late 1970s and '80s she had had a creditable career in subversive political activism, was a regular visitor to the anti-American protest at Greenham Common and undertook Cruise Watches, when at night she parked up in a lay-by in wait for a missile to emerge from its bunker, hopefully on an exercise and not to start World War 3, and head into the English countryside to set up for a test firing. My mum's mission was to rush to a phone box, inform other members of the Cruise Watch telephone tree, all on land lines of course, and then tail the nuclear missile and if necessary disrupt its firing. Very annoyingly none ever emerged from Greenham when my mum was in the lay-by with her Thermos and – no doubt – well-thought-out picnic. I would have liked to have heard her story of how she averted a nuclear holocaust in the dead of night in some Berkshire village by wrestling with a man on top of a tank armed with nothing more than a Cox's Orange Pippin in a string bag.

Susie was definitely at some point being watched by the CIA. In the 1980s the phone at home was tapped, but as so often with US military interventions, it didn't go quite to plan. When you picked up the receiver you could hear old conversations being replayed, with Americans commenting over them.

Somewhere on a computer chip deep under the Pentagon there was probably a file on my mother. Albeit a slim one. She certainly claimed there was, and it was a matter of pride to her. Quite how I could persuade the CIA to dig it out, review it and see her as a security threat so great that she required termination with extreme prejudice, I wasn't certain.

In the 1980s Susie joined the Campaign Against the Arms Trade, and then led the Fairford Peace Group. I say led, because its constitution was precisely the kind of dictatorship that the Group was committed to eradicating elsewhere in the world. She still subscribed forty years later to the *Campaign Against Arms Trade* magazine, surely the most hopeful and hopeless publication ever produced. It has the very annoying feature of looking from a distance like an old copy of *Private Eye*, and many times I smiled to see it in Susie's downstairs toilet but ended staring at headlines like: STOPPING THE WORLD ARMS TRADE. PROGRESS SO FAR. And DONATE TODAY! (I have not added the exclamation mark.)

Fairford was the Gloucestershire village where we lived; it had a huge US airbase on its outskirts. It was during the Kissinger years and the US had a policy of keeping armed nuclear warheads in the air round the clock in case of a strike on the US, or, I suppose, the UK. The tankers that refuelled these bombers took off from Fairford at all hours of the day and night, and Susie argued, quite reasonably, that it placed our sleepy little Cotswold village high up the Kremlin's list of targets. She was never overawed by a challenge, and she decided, with her peace group, five timid locals, to reverse US global military policy and get the base closed down.

Once a year, to distract the public, the Americans and the Ministry of Defence put on an air show, ostensibly for the RAF Benevolent Fund, featuring the Red Arrows and other acrobatic aircraft, which drew thousands of spectators to the base. On the far side of the runway a lot of boozed-up politicians from distant, repressive regimes turned up to buy armaments under cover of this fun day out for all the family. Objective number two of the Fairford Peace Group, after defeating the Pentagon, was to disrupt the air show and stop the arms fair. Susie devised a plan. This is what I was saying about how she had changed. She had said to me 'I was a bit of a mouse before your father died.' That had changed. 'I discovered that widows were on their own, second-class citizens,' she continued, 'and while I think men should be the leaders, if you haven't got a man, you have to do it yourself.'

My father died in winter. He was killed in a car crash on 23 December 1968. He was driving home for Christmas. The line in the cheesy Christmas song has always hurt me to hear. I guess because I hear him saying it. Anyway, we kids got the news on Christmas Eve. I remember looking at the presents around the tree and seeing ones for him, and wanted to move them, in case they reminded Mum that Daddy was dead.

We had a skiing holiday booked in the New Year and didn't cancel it. I approved of that. I felt that by the day after his death, the time for mourning was over. It was a holiday – it was Christmas! – and therefore we should all be happy. It set the marker for grieving in the Kennaway family. You just bloody well get on with life. But I have little recollection of the skiing holiday. I was stunned. On the first anniversary of his death Susie decided to take us on safari. It was planned as a diversionary exercise

I imagine, and was well intended. But while we were there something happened. The transformation of my mum. From mouse to international political militant on a CIA watch list.

We trundled down dusty tracks, looking at animals by day and at night stayed in a good hotel perched on the lip of the Ngorongoro Crater. The dining room was cantilevered over a huge drop and had a breathtaking view of the herds of animals on the valley floor a quarter of a mile away. At meal times the Kennaway family, my mum and four kids between 9 and 15, were led by the maitre d' through the dining room to a table at the back with a view of the dumpsters and air-conditioning units. I must emphasise that this happened in 1969, which was a different era. Now sexism in Kenya is probably much worse. Susie, after a couple of days of being directed to this table, stopped the maitre d' as he turned from his lectern to direct us to our gloomy corner, and said 'No. We are going to sit over there ...'

She pointed to an unoccupied table by the plate-glass window overlooking the teeming herds of wildebeests and flocks of flamingos.

'I am sorry. That table is reserved,' he said. 'Please follow me madam.'

'Stop,' she said. 'The fact that I am a woman unaccompanied by a man does not give you the right to give me the worst table in the restaurant. We are going to sit over there. Follow me children.'

She then marched the four of us through the dining room and told us to sit down. I expect I was a bit hangdog. The whole restaurant muttered as we passed. A woman without a man! Possibly divorced. Demanding proper service! The very cheek of it. The maitre d' with his tiny bow tie hurried after us, and told us again that the table was reserved. I happened to know by whom because I had seen them: an airline pilot and his gleaming family. I have him chisel jawed in a pale blue safari suit with a wide belt sewn onto the jacket. He was travelling with three children but no spouse. I stood up.

'Sit down,' my mother said. And to the maitre d' she said 'Can you bring us some menus, please?'

The maitre d' was the undisputed big beast of the dining room, but was being told what to do by a female of the species. Now I see it as courageous and beautiful, but at the time I was ashamed of her. The airline pilot later that evening asked my mum for a dance while we kids larked around in the lifts and the lobby. I watched Susie waltzing with this strange man and thought *Great, maybe she'll marry him and we'll be a normal family again.*

Soon after, Susie discovered we weren't as rich as my father said we were and she set about starting a business: a restaurant called Pinks, in Fairford, Gloucestershire, where she employed only women, and made a point of always giving women the best tables.

So the Maitre d' in the Ngorongoro Crater Hotel was the first to meet the irresistible force that Susie became as a widow. Many more met the same fate. Men who thought they could overlook her and ignore her. Men who found out they were wrong.

One such person was Mr Melville-Ross. His name sticks in my memory forty years later. He had the misfortune to be the chairman of the Nationwide Building Society, which sponsored the RAF Air Tattoo. My mother's plan to sabotage the air show and arms fair possessed her trademark meticulousness. She hounded Melville-Ross in every way she could. She co-ordinated a pinpoint bombardment of letters accusing him of abetting war crimes, and organised a mass withdrawal of funds by customers of his bank. He eventually cancelled the sponsorship. I have no doubt that despite the passage of time, and however doddery Mr Melville-Ross is now, the words *Susie Kennaway* whispered in his ear would give him a nasty start.

A second front in Susie's war against the Tattoo involved dragooning the members of the peace group and anyone else she could conscript, i.e. us children (though I managed to desert), to infiltrate the air show posing as employees and hand out pamphlets which looked – at first sight – like official programmes, but which were in fact subversive publications designed and written by Susie, featuring gruesome images and harsh facts about war. Susie made everyone dress in white shirts and black trousers and personally sewed shoulder bags so her little army would look convincing.

The following year I was pressganged into the ranks. This time Susie made placards which featured a drawing of a child splattered with blood holding up their hands, under which was written THE ONLY ARMS WE NEED. The members of the peace group plus me and my three siblings were lined up on the roadside (a specific distance apart) and made to shake this hard-core image of a child with its head torn off at the cars queuing to enter the air show.

At the pre-demo briefing Susie gave the order for us to shout 'Shame! Shame on you!' as we stood on the verge, but the peace group were mainly quite shy people, and *my* heart was certainly not in the project. I was 18, and quite wanted to go in and have a look at the aeroplanes. We all ended up just mumbling something quietly unless she was watching us. I remember standing in burning summer heat – it may have been the 1976 scorcher – being shouted at by men crawling past in their cars. I let my placard drop into the grass and tried to saunter back home but you couldn't get round Susie that easily and she made me pick it up and get back in position. It was a ghastly day. One small child was so alarmed at the placard he burst into tears and a mother yelled at me that I had ruined their day out.

So ... all I had to do was anonymously inform the CIA that my mum, who, I would tell them, had fled from Fairford to avoid being questioned for anti-American military sabotage in the 1970s, had resurfaced in France and was up to her old tricks again. My mum had donated all the documents relating to the activities of the Fairford Peace Group to the Faculty of Peace Studies at Bradford University. If the Americans had no records of her – it just made her more code red. Telephone intercepts would prove she was trying to get hold of a poison. Her target? Who knew? I had once seen a picture of Henry Kissinger on holiday in the South of France, maybe I could say her plan was to settle an old score. With any luck President Trump's CIA wouldn't think twice about liquidating her. Then I wouldn't have to worry.

SIX

A good innings

WITH DEATH ON MY mind, I snatched the chance of going to a funeral as soon as one came up. It didn't take long. A friend said they were coming in so thick and fast she had two funerals clash on one afternoon. My friend Phil Dirtbox told me he had two cremations in a row, so half the congregation stayed in place while they wheeled in the new coffin and close family members. My girlfriend Amanda's granny Pat had died in a residential care home in Altrincham, Manchester. Amanda was much closer to her other granny, Nanna, but we made the journey up to the crematorium, she to support her dad, and me to feast on death, close up.

We arrived at Amanda's dad's house. Paul, her father, was keeping a lid on his emotions by meticulously organising events, including timing the order of service and repeating: 'It's not a sad death. She was 97. It's not sad at all really. She was 97... Amy, you've got three minutes twenty seconds for that Rabbie Burns poem.'

We left the house and drove out of the suburbs into the country on a narrow winding lane. There was plenty of traffic coming in the other direction, and when I saw it included an empty hearse I realised it was the last service leaving. We passed a village hall with men standing outside in ill-fitting suits and I said 'That must be the place', but it turned out to be yet another funeral party.

We drove on a few miles and soon after a farmyard turned onto the generous tarmac of the crematorium, which looked to me as though it had been built on land sold by the farmer. He probably thought he was getting a good deal until he realised how busy his road was going to get with the country's changing demographic.

Parking was tight. Crematorium design doesn't seem to attract the most creative architects. There was no hint of Iranian genius or Spanish flair about this miserable brick bungalow that had all the elan of a sewage works.

We arrived late, but they hadn't gone in. The teenage grandchildren were dressed in black, which for them meant nightclub clothes, and this did add some welcome glamour. I had seen this before at another funeral, but that was a very different kind of event, and nobody thought of glamour then. Between glances at his watch, Paul issued orders to the pall-bearers and informed us where we were sitting. I wouldn't have to worry about any of this, because Susie would without a shadow of a doubt have already made all her own funeral arrangements. She had been going over in her mind who gets in her front pew for the past ten years. She was no doubt working on the impromptu eulogy that one of her acolytes (not me) would – spontaneously – be unable to hold in. Nothing would be left to chance. The only reason I didn't know the details was because I had a policy of not talking about any arrangements for *after* Susie's death, as they inevitably allowed her to lead me into a conversation about her will, one of her favourite hobbies. She loved to inform anyone about who was getting a little bit more and who a little bit less, and precisely why. I was convinced the whole thing was a set-up. No will probably existed: she just got her fun describing one when she was bored. And as far as I could tell from their lifestyle, there wouldn't be anything left, particularly if she and Stanley were set on becoming coke-heads.

It was cold outside the crematorium. The portico looked like something Marshal Tito would appear under. I heard that the first guests to arrive were asked if they were there for Violet's funeral, and they naturally said no, because they didn't know that Violet preferred all her life to be called Pat. That struck me as a strange decision, but I liked being told about it because I got an authentic glimpse into her character, a woman I had never met, and realistically was unlikely to as she was at that moment being lifted in a varnished box onto six shoulders under Paul's close supervision.

Gaiety is deadly at a funeral, whether forced or natural, and surely more depressing than just being sad. There was a live choir which sang gospel and some show-tunes that Granny Pat liked. The celebrant was clearly a refugee from show-biz. She struck an upbeat but respectful tone, led the choir, and gave us a lung-busting solo in We'll Meet Again, but surpassed herself when she misread the order of service and asked Amy to come forward and recite a poem by a Jewish man of the cloth called Rabbi Burns.

Paul stood proudly out front and gave an account of Granny Pat's life that I admired because it seemed to me honest. Her two failed marriages for instance, and forgotten stepchildren, were featured in the narrative. There would be no mention of Brian, my mum's colourful, disruptive and disobedient second husband at her funeral, that was for certain. I'm sure it will be clearly stated in her will who gives her eulogy. I'd be surprised if any of us will ever even have met the poor sap.

Granny Pat died aged 97 and all agreed had had a good innings. Though 97, three short of a century, would actually be called by any cricketer an unlucky innings. Nowadays good innings are usually in the 300s. Her demise was swift and elegant. One moment she was gaily entertaining grandchildren in her room at the care home and then she lost control of her bowels, was hospitalised, diagnosed with a tumour, put on morphine, and died a week later. My ears pricked up when Paul said 'She was asking to die at the end.' That sounded familiar. Everyone in the congregation thought it a reasonable request. I knew then that I didn't think Susie's was.

I am not sure how you would describe Susie's innings. She certainly hogged the crease, and survived quite a few appeals. She just wasn't – yet at least – the kind of batswoman to signal to the pavilion that she was ready for a declaration, even if she was on 87. And if given out by the umpire I have no doubt that she would have called for a referral to the TMO and stood her ground until every spectator was slow handclapping her.

As we filed out into the whipping Cheshire wind, I remembered the last funeral I had attended: an absolutely heart-breaking occasion on a warm summer day, for my cousin's 21 year old son. He had killed himself over a lost love. He too had asked for it, but none thought his request legitimate. Granny Pat's funeral was not like Barney's. Outside the Altrincham Crem the youngsters high fived each other, because to them death was a distant event, rather as we had all thought it should rightfully have been for Barney.

I wandered around the back of the building for a cigarette on my own. Death made me want to smoke. It should have a warning on it. I found a skip full of cut flowers in cellophane and twisted wreaths spelling out GRANDAD and MUM. I have so many times stood in front of a piece of art that purported to be about death and always felt entirely unmoved, or rather unconvinced. But this discarded collection of what I believe are termed floral tributes, many I am sure sent from people who were not at some ill-attended service in the crematorium, spoke to me of the futility of doing anything graceful or meaningful in the face of death. Flowers in cellophane? Who thought that up? Who honestly believed that a man grieving his son would be consoled by a bunch of petunias that would end up petals-down in a skip in a service bay next to a broken-down car, some planking and a cracked urinal?

A tarmac path wound in a sickly curve between garish trees, strange bushes and concrete ornaments, as though the challenge was to create the most unnatural environment possible. Maybe the garden of remembrance's function was to console those newly bereaved by making them remember how ugly life could be.

Speeding towards the wake and our first drink, we nearly had a head on with a hearse, this one fully loaded. If we had crashed – and god forbid there had been fatalities – we would have been described by the crematorium as passing trade.

After the party we shambled, plastered, back to Paul and Paula's house to do some more serious drinking while the youngsters went off to the gym. Paul was an Immigration Appeals Court Judge, and a few of his old muckers who came back to drink around the kitchen table were lawyers. In a gap in the conversation, I said 'My mother has asked me to help her kill herself. Oh, and her husband.'

David, an engaging criminal lawyer, a small man with a sparkle in his eyes and a well polished joke always near his lips stared at me. 'Don't do it,' he said, suddenly not drunk. 'It's murder. You are an accessory. Before the fact. No matter what the circumstances are, I couldn't get you less than life.'

Paul asked 'Have you considered taking her to a country where it's legal? Like Switzerland?'

'I did mention Switzerland to her,' I replied. 'But there's too much red tape. What if I just quietly scored 4 grams of heroin and slipped it in her coffee? No one would know.'

'You could get busted buying it. Possession with intent to supply.'

'Not necessarily,' said another drunken lawyer, or he could have been a judge. I was playing with fire here. 'You could argue that it was intended for personal use. That would reduce your sentence considerably.'

'But he would have to bring some evidence.'

'You would have ask your mother to testify it was to kill her. But that could raise issues in itself.'

They all started laughing, and I felt it was at my expense.

SEVEN

The man in the loft

A S GRANNY PAT'S FINAL decline was quick and easy, Granny Nanna's, Amanda's maternal grandmother, was proving to be the opposite. The day after Granny Pat's funeral, fighting our way through heavy traffic and a blinding hangover, we cut across countless northern towns and bypasses to Nottingham to visit Nanna in her care home.

Only a year before Nanna had been living in the postwar detached house in a working-class Salford suburb that she had moved into with her new husband Eric in 1947. She was a minuscule woman, no more than 4 foot 6, with thin ginger hair and stick-like limbs, who kept her house spick and span, though redolent of 70 years of accumulated Embassy cigarette smoke. On flying visits Amanda would cram her freezer with meals for one, and go and ask the neighbours to keep an eye on her. Nanna didn't seem to have any friends of her own. Since Eric had died it had emerged how controlling a husband he had been. Long-withheld stories of his intransigence and meanness spilled out. She told Amanda she had married the wrong man.

'Don't marry the tinsel instead of the gold,' she said. I feared she was referring to me. 'Like I did.'

Nanna's husband had worn her down to papery meekness. Even after he died she didn't have the confidence to get out of the house and pursue new interests. She had a daughter, Amanda's mum, but she had died of alcoholism 25 years ago, and it looked to me like – on top of everything else – the shame and pain of that had never fully faded. Mike and Amanda, her only grandchildren, had made new lives away from Salford. Nanna had only one reliable friend left: the TV. Well, that, and the cold-callers from the double-glazing, broadband and scamming industries, for whom she was easy pickings.

Amanda grew worried when Nanna, who had saved money all her life, said that a nice builder called Nicky Thomas was going to fix her gutters for only four thousand five hundred pounds. He had even given her a discount. The day Thomas drew up in his dilapidated and filthy van the neighbours kindly told him to bugger off before they called the Police. Nanna also got involved with negotiating quite a few complex telephone and TV packages but I think drove the salesmen so mad that they gave up on her before they could close a lucrative mis-sale. But she always sent Amanda £100 on her birthday and at Christmas, in a card which Amanda opened in a wave of guilt because she didn't spend more time with her. It was another difficult consequence of her mum dying. The responsibility for caring had jumped a generation and Nanna really didn't want to be a burden on a forty-year-old grandchild with her own twelve-year-old son.

Things started to get more worrying when Nanna said that the man in the television was telling her there was someone upstairs, and that she couldn't fully explain who he was or what he was doing because the man in the television would be angry with her for talking to Amanda. Amanda got in touch with Social Services and we made the four-hour drive from Somerset to see Nanna with the team leader. Nanna was confused and on a loop about the man listening in, whose powers were increasing because he could now turn over the TV channel and make her watch things she didn't want to see. Amanda ran through the controls on the handset for the twentieth time, but it was hopeless. Such things were beyond Nanna.

Already shrunken, she was now frighteningly emaciated, though her deep-socket eyes lit up as she gazed with adoration at the granddaughter she hardly ever saw. It was painful for Amanda to see how much she was missed. But Amanda couldn't go and live in Salford. Her son Haruka was at school in Somerset and Amanda had a shop in Glastonbury. It was impossible. And Amanda couldn't house Nanna with her down South. She had just moved into my house, and even if she hadn't, she was out all day working in the shop and away three months a year manufacturing clothes in India and Nepal. She had to make do with phone conversations which had to be shouted and repeated because Nanna couldn't get her hearing aid to work. Nanna told Amanda, how fed up she was.

'I've lived my life Amanda, and you've got little Haruka. I don't want to be any more trouble than I already am. But it's the bloody man in the TV again. He's not leaving me alone. He can talk to me from the loft. I've got to go up and check. Nicky Thomas telephoned. Did I tell you? He said he could probably help. But I'm that tired Amanda. I'm that bloody tired I don't know if I want to go on, Amanda. Can you hear me? It's that bloody man, he's hearing what I'm saying. Did you hear what he said? Did I tell you he changes the channel on the telly? I've called them at Sky that many times and I've told Debbie – she's ever so nice – but she said there weren't nothing she could do as it didn't fall under the warranty. Imagine that! There's a man in me bloody TV and it's not covered. Warranties, they never work when you need them.'

A week later we got a call from Rita, a neighbour, to tell us that Nanna had fallen down the stairs and been taken by ambulance to hospital, where she was in a highly confused state. When Amanda got back from seeing her, she was distraught. Nanna hadn't recognised her. She didn't know where she was or even quite who she was. She had wet her bed and lost her slippers.

Through tears, Amanda said, 'When I finally got through to her she said "Amanda! Oh Amanda! Oh I'm so happy to see you. Thank you for coming. I've been so worried about you. Where is this place? Why am I here? I want to go home and die, Amanda, I don't like this place".'

Amanda tried to get her discharged, but the doctors weren't having any of it. Amanda and her brother Mike explained quietly to them that Nanna wanted to go home and die. The doctors said they couldn't let that happen. Exasperated, the best Amanda and Mike could get was a DO NOT RESUSCITATE order, and hope for pneumonia.

To me the decision to keep Nanna in hospital seemed inhumane and cruel, not to mention extravagant and crazy and lots of other things, all bad. Here is a small statistic for all taxpayers to consider: on average, 40 per cent of a person's medical costs are spent in the last six months of their life. (This figure is disputed. Some think it's too low, others too high. My advice is to do your own research.) All this money being wasted on Nanna, keeping her in torment against her will could have been spent on getting better treatment for a child with cancer. Nanna got a urinary infection, which was standard for geriatrics in hospital, and Amanda took her son out of school to drive up for what we thought would be their last goodbye. But when she got there, she found Nanna sitting up in bed. The doctors had prescribed antibiotics and she was responding well.

Two weeks later Nanna was deemed ready for discharge, but not back home, because the assessment by Salford Social Services was that her home, with no toilet on the ground floor, and Nanna unable to manage stairs, was not fit for her habitation. They were looking to supply a bed and a chemical commode for Nanna to use downstairs, and arrange for care workers to drop by to check she was OK twice a day. We knew that Nanna, already deeply confused and weak after her infection, would not be able to deal with this arrangement. The image of the poor old woman sitting on a plastic chemical toilet in the brown tinted hallway was unbearable. The idea of Nanna going home quietly to die was now looking horribly messy. It was one thing her being allowed to die there, but sending her back to a lonely demise with a chemical commode didn't seem right. It crossed a line.

There followed a wrangle with the Council, basically over money. If Nanna was placed in a care home, the Council would only pay five weeks before Nanna would have to stump up the £2000.00 a month it cost. Nanna had worked for 60 years to pay off her mortgage and save £10,000. In five months a life's worth of thrift would be wiped out, and soon after that her modest home – which she had longed to leave to her two grandchildren, to give them a foot on the property ladder – would be sold and bit by bit handed over to the government to whom she had paid *all* her taxes *all* her life in the belief they would look after her in her old age.

A few friends said there were some scams to get round the Council taking the money from Nanna's house to pay for her care. It did seem iniquitous that those who hadn't saved anything were getting the same care as those who had put something aside all their lives.

But Amanda and Mike accepted their fate: they were probably not going to get their deposits for a home of their own. They resigned themselves to losing it all, because the alternative seemed to be wishing Nanna would die for pecuniary rather than humane reasons. And they didn't want to do that.

So Nanna was put into care in Salford, and her first words when Amanda and I went to visit were 'Are you Lois?' She had lost her false teeth and her hearing aid was broken.

'No Nanna, I'm Amanda,' Amanda said, kneeling by her chair and stroking her sparse hair. 'It's me. Amanda.'

She darted a look at me. 'Who's that horrible man?' she snapped. 'Standing there like that. It's not Mike is it?'

'No Nanna, that's Guy.'

'Who's Guy? Get him out of here. I don't like him.'

I left the room and looked around the place. It was a two-storey modern purpose-built building with wide fire doors and a dozen bedrooms off a day room where the patients sat, some with children or spouses struggling with anguished conversation.

A woman came in with a little cake and card. 'Happy birthday darling,' she said to a man, who looked at her blankly. 'How old are you? Can you remember?'

I could see what was going on here. They were losing their minds, and one or two strikingly early. There was a man not much older than me being served tea by a nurse while doing a commentary on a cricket match in his head. I didn't want to sit down for fear of being mistaken for a patient by another visitor, and given the kindly but anxious smile that I had been dishing out. I went back to Nanna's room with its view of a roughly mown lawn, Larchlap fence and leylandii; Amanda cradled Nanna's head in her lap stroking her hair in the most tender and loving way conceivable. Nanna's eyes were closed, and her brittle body in repose.

'I don't know Amanda ...' Nanna was saying. 'I don't know whether I am living or dying. I don't know. My hair's a bloody mess. I'm a mess. I've gone to pot. I don't know. I don't bloody know any more.'

The drive to Salford was simply too much for Amanda and Mike to do every week, so it was decided that Nanna would move to a care home either in Somerset or Nottingham, where Mike lived with his young family. Characteristically, both siblings said they wanted her close by, and would therefore bear the brunt of the work, so we all started to look at care homes.

Here are a few facts I discovered reading Atul Gawande's sobering *Being Mortal,* a book about ageing: In 1900 life expectancy was under 50. Today it is over 90 if you are a Korean woman, and not much less if you are a Brit. In the mid-1800s the average family size was 7. It is now just over 3. We all know parents and offspring used to live together in the family nest. Now just 10 per cent of Europeans over 80 live with their kids. This means there are a lot of wrinklies needing to be looked after by very few children, who don't live anywhere near them. Hence the care-home industry. We are doing what social scientists call 'intimacy at a distance'. Or at least you lot are. I called my mum about once a month and was plotting to kill her.

EIGHT

Deep-sea fishing for mackerel

T HE TERM 'RETIREMENT COMMUNITY' was coined in the 1960s in Phoenix, Arizona. It basically meant a place to bung the parents which didn't make you feel too guilty. Not surprisingly, they caught on.

It was not for another twenty years that nurses, doctors, patients and relatives – everyone, basically – noticed that retirement homes made their occupants miserable. The next generation of institution was called 'assisted living' and was pioneered in Oregon by a nurse and entrepreneur called Keren Wilson in 1980. Wilson argued that the care homes were basically set up to maximise the health and safety of the occupants and minimise work for the owners. They were holding-pens for old people, whose lives were reduced to the absolute minimum acceptable to their children and legislation. A small room, a TV, two photographs and a wardrobe. Keren made the startling observation that the same thing that made life worth living for young people, did the same for old. It turned out whatever our age, we all wanted to fully live our lives rather than simply exist. And she said '*Let's let these geriatrics have pets and visitors if and when they want to, and go to bed and get up whenever suits them.*' If they wanted to lie in all day, that was fine, Keren said. Let them. They were old enough to know what they wanted. And she advocated giving them a door that only they could lock, from both sides. Privacy, and a degree of self-determination had been removed from their lives to suit the staff rota, basically. Keren also insisted that the occupants of her homes be given kitchens and the freedom to cook what they wanted. That meant the oldies were going to be in possession of a knife, which of course ran against all the instincts of the managers, who had stripped anything that might cause a problem, including the old people's personalities, out of their system.

The experiment was a success. Doctors made the not-so-extraordinary discovery that if you gave old people a degree of joy, creativity and choice, they didn't decay and decline so catastrophically. It turned out that three hours a week of crochet, bingo and arm yoga was not sufficient to make them want to go on living. And I didn't blame them. Some places took Keren Wilson's theory further. A bored and clever care-home doctor in New York called Bill Thomas introduced dogs, cats and 100 parakeets into his care home and – surprise, surprise – it encouraged the occupants to be less reliant on drugs and live longer, because they had to deal with the responsibilities and rewards of caring for these animals.

The problem was that creating a building that was full of the unpredictability and challenges of a genuine domestic home was all a bit too much like hard work for the care-home owners. The staff I had seen at Nanna's Salford care home didn't seem to be up for it at all. They looked overweight and bored. They carefully did the minimum required to keep their job and stay out of trouble. Their sensitivity was reserved not for the patients but for their own employment rights. I had watched a table of staff on their break drinking mugs of instant coffee, checking their watches and ignoring the patients, before heaving themselves onto their ostentatiously flat shoes and shlepping off to do the next thing only because it had to be done.

I started designing my own old people's home, based on Wilson's, Thomas' and my own principles of what made life worth living. I pictured a large ramshackle country mansion by the sea with a big lawn out front and greenhouse and weedy veg garden out back. The decor was fading-country-house: beautiful threadbare rugs, well worn classic English furniture and open fires with baskets of split logs that occupants could pick up and throw on the grate.

There were no fire doors, and no emergency signage anywhere. In fact there were no signs of any kind, because signs mean authority. There was a swimming pool, jacuzzi, steam room and sauna, all open round the clock, none with lifeguards giving orders. Masseurs were available whenever you wanted one.

In the drawing room the drinks tray was well stocked. The nurses' job was not to purée my dinner but to fill the goddam ice bucket and get that tricky champagne cork off.

Activities included deep-sea fishing for mackerel – life jackets optional. *But someone might fall in.* Yes indeed. But as I will have survived for eighty years doing more or less exactly what I wanted, I think I know more about my own safety than some care professional. Also popular would be picnics close to the cliff edge and trips to the local race course or dog track. Drugs would be on tap, but not the type prescribed by some pipsqueak doctor in a white coat. The purveyor of drugs to my care home would I very much hope be wearing leather trousers, have neck tattoos and sell us occupants whatever we needed or wanted, the two not being synonymous. I come from a generation that knows more about drugs than any medical doctor that I have encountered. I want cocaine, on occasion, a good pipe of hash when called for, and a tab of acid from time to time to do with my mates in the day room, or, if sunny, lying on cushions on thick Persian rugs on the lawn. Culturally, we would have talks from leading (not local) authors and film-makers. In a top-of-the-range screening room we'd watch some good movies, the choice of which the staff would have absolutely

NO say in. We would go to the theatre from time to time. Not some lame local production, but the RSC or The National. There would be ample spare rooms for visits of any length by friends and family. Everyone would have a double bed, linen sheets and goose-down pillows. Six of them. And the bed would go up and down by electric motor. We would submit to no medical tests or surveys unless we requested them. The doctor would be someone we gave orders to, not the other way round. The only concessions to decrepitude I could think of apart from the electric beds was that there should be a lift.

NINE

Over the rainbow

MIKE WON THE TUSSLE of the care home and Nanna was placed in one near him called 'Lifehaven', where a vacancy had just come up. An ominous phrase, which I refrained from remarking on. There are some incredibly good care homes in Britain, but Nanna was not in one of them. Smack opposite HM Prison Nottingham, 'Lifehaven' was a modern brick building on a busy intersection, with narrow corridors and low ceilings. It was to this place that we crawled through traffic and hangovers after Granny Pat's funeral.

I got an email from Susie. She wrote at the end *'Any progress on the elephant in the room?'*

That could have meant anything with our family. So much went on and so little was acknowledged that we basically grew up in an elephant enclosure. But in this case I knew what she meant.

From the very beginning I had wondered whether she had been serious. *I* hadn't been completely serious. It was a joke to me, bumping her off. But now she was chasing me up on the project. Perhaps it wasn't a joke to her. Though maybe it was a ploy to pull me towards her, and get some filial attention? It was true that over many years I had – out of suspicion – withdrawn to what I considered a safe distance, i.e. about a thousand miles.

I had in the past few months begun to understand her wish. I could now see a good argument for cutting from the script of life the last painful, bewildering and humiliating act in its entirety. I had to admit that killing yourself in a manner and at a time of your own choice, to escape gathering dementia and/or chronic agonising pain, made some sense. Who wanted a life lived in hot airless rooms with ever more infrequent and meaning-less visits from strangers who insisted they were your family? Every sane middle-aged person has a fear of ending up slumped in a plastic wingback chair in a circle of other gaga geriatrics, while some failed actor tries to get them to sing *Over the Rainbow*.

As we waited to be admitted to 'Lifehaven', we had to sign a register, because of, I believe, fire-safety regulations, as if this paper book would somehow sur-vive any conflagration. Or, with the building going up in flames, the chief fireman would lick his thumb and go slowly through the pages and say 'hang on. Someone didn't sign out last Thursday. That man there! Go back in and look for him.'

The fire door clicked open to reveal an anxious elderly woman in her coat with handbag and cigs looking like she was about to nip out for a fag. A large woman with short straight blond hair pulled her back. Apparently she stood there all day trying to slip out. Escape was on the minds of those on both sides of the road.

Keren Wilson's research had not been totally ignored. The doors to the bedrooms that lined the corridor were brightly painted in primary colours and featured numbers and knockers to make them look like front doors of real homes. But that was about it. With sinking heart I entered the day room. It was an unpromising polygon with two concrete pillars in the middle and a view of the traffic through one window and a scruffy patch of grass through another. I looked around at the nodding heads and gaping mouths, feeling the torpor grip me.

A man in a collarless shirt and grey braces inched past me on a frame mumbling to himself. He wasn't the kind of person you wanted to ask 'How are you?' to.

Nanna had been there three months, and I was not expecting her to recognise us. But she raised a tiny feeble hand and croaked 'I'm over here!' And as we came close she said 'I'm so glad you came Amanda. I'm so happy to see you.' She eyed me suspiciously. 'Did he have to come with you?' she asked.

While we made a clumsy half-sitting, half-standing group around her, Nanna started introducing us to the other patients. 'That's Arthur.' An old man with wispy white hair and a huge nose stared at us from his wingback. 'He's gone fragile in his legs. His mind is perfect. Isn't it Arthur?'

Arthur waved warmly.

'He lived in a respite care home in Knutsford, didn't you? He pays every week. That's Marjorie. She checks the doors and tidies up. That's Ilene. We don't talk unless we have to. This is my Amanda, I told you about ...' she beamed from her sunken, toothless face. I noticed murmurs of recognition and approval from the patients, and a couple of the staff came through and said hello to us.

'We know all about you, Amanda,' said another visitor, 'your granny is the life and soul of the day room. She's always telling us about you. You have a shop, yes?'

I sat down, and watched, astonished.

I thought Nanna would be dying, but here she was holding Amanda's hand, crying with happiness.

It wasn't over at all.

Over the next few weeks Mike phoned in with progress reports. 'She's at last getting the social life she was denied by that husband. She's been scared to come out of her house for 60 years and now she's got the chance to make some friends and have some fun. It's bloody brilliant. She's lapping it up. She's even got a boyfriend: Craig the handyman. He adores her. They've got her on protein shakes and she's put on five pounds. She's basically bald but I haven't seen her this healthy for years and she acts like she's Diana Dors.'

I remembered a few of the things I had said only months ago about it being best for all if Nanna were allowed to die. I hoped Mike and Amanda had forgotten them.

Nanna's house had meanwhile been sold. They got 120 grand for it. One-hundred-and-twenty weeks, or three years, of care-home bills.

'We can forget about getting any cash from the house, worst luck,' Mike laughed. 'At this rate she's going to go on for years. It wouldn't surprise me if she entered herself for the Manchester half marathon.'

Old people's porn

I COULD SEE THAT SUSIE could not cope with Stanley and the 5 kg wheelchair for too long, and nor, realistically, was she ever going to deal with a care home. There was a moment to consider elegantly Signing Off, but it didn't seem as though it had yet arrived. After reading about care homes and geriatric psychology I had decided it was way too early to contemplate suicide for her and Stanley. It was not time to go. We just had to find a way for the two of them to live that was neither in neglect nor in an institution.

My thoughts turned to the barn conversion I was doing beside my house. The idea was to tenant it and make some extra cash. It was a large space with a mezzanine level accessed only by steep, geriatric-proof stairs.

Drunk, I googled *"domestic lifts and stairlifts"*. Old people's porn. I knew where I was headed: assisted living. And I was going to be the assister.

Was I really going to invite them to come and live beside me? Could I really do it? Could I hobble my life for her? This whole thing, my taking an interest in her, which was meant to hasten her departure, and had been for a strictly six-month maximum time limit, had badly backfired. I had started thinking about her life, and communicating with her about it, and this is where it had led me: I was going to end up her as my neighbour. And, inevitably, I'd end up like all previous neighbours: in court being grilled by her barrister.

But I knew how stubborn she was, and I knew also that the move to the UK would – without a shadow of a doubt – be perceived as a retreat and loss of face. After all those hours and hours of telling everyone how washed up Britain is and how civilised life in France is, it was going to be hard to finesse a move to Somerset.

I decided to visit her and go over the options. I made plans to see her in April, and I strongly suspected that she thought I was going to turn up with a vial of hemlock. In fact all I was going to have in my pocket was a catalogue of stairlifts.

ELEVEN

Spiders in the mouth

Hi Guy,
I don't know if you are aware but I spoke to
Mummy, who had just returned from hospital
and she has a blood-poisoning issue that may be
very serious. At present she is back from the hos-
pital, resting in bed awaiting blood-test results.
She asked me not to tell Jane.

THAT WAS FROM MY brother. I called France. It
rang for a long time before Susie answered. She
sounded unusually weak. She liked to present a confident tone on the phone. A few years ago she had a
car accident and ended up upside down in a ditch. It
was the fault of the surface of the road. Suspended by
her seat belt she managed to find her phone, and after
trying one or two other people, called me in the UK. She
asked after my kids, and whether they had received their
birthday presents, there being a thank-you letter sub-
text. She spoke for at least five minutes before I asked
her how she was and – *slowly* – it came to light that
she was hanging upside down in a ditch. She said she

really didn't want to bother me but could I get hold of someone to come and help her. I said one word, and it was all OK: pompiers.

This time I brushed off talk of the trellis being blown off the terrace and the solution to this problem, and asked her how she was.

'I am ill actually,' she said in a tender, vulnerable voice, which I knew to be a terrifying state for her to be caught in. I got a fleeting glimpse of the girl who had endured an appalling childhood neglected by her parents during the war. 'They haven't found what it is, but they say it is an unusually aggressive infection, sending my body into trauma. I was taken by ambulance to hospital last week, all totally unnecessary. They did a lot of tests and I said I would go home. I wasn't going to stay there.' The adult Susie was taking back control.

A superbug. Not something to put my mind at rest.

'How are you feeling now?'

'I haven't eaten anything for six days, so I've lost some weight. Bit of a bore as it's made me terribly weak. The doctor came twice. She's so nice and so friendly and has got so much time that she stayed for half an hour.'

She can't be that bad, I thought to myself, she can still get a swipe at the NHS in.

'This is a right bugger as it's come at the wrong time,' she continued.

When is the right time for a superbug? I didn't say.

'Right in the middle of the replanting scheme.' She paused and lowered her voice. 'We simply must make arrangements. Stanley couldn't remember where the torch was and he had forgotten where the light switch is. I slept for five days, and he had to try and look after me. It was a terrible mess. He kept spilling things on the carpet and all my nighties were dirty because he couldn't find the washing machine. I was afraid to wake up because of what's happened. There was this terrible smell. From inside me … I had terrible dreams of spiders coming up my throat and men stealing babies.'

Stan couldn't find the washing machine. Mum dreaming of spiders in her mouth in dirty night clothes.

'That sounds awful,' I said. 'I'm so sorry I wasn't there. You should have rung me.'

'I didn't want to worry you. Anyway I'm fine. And you mustn't tell Jane.'

'Why?' Jane, my sister, was a musician who had a part-time job in geriatric care to make ends meet.

'I don't want her dropping everything and coming over here. She must earn money.'

'I think Jane would want to know.'

'No!'

'She cares about you. When people love you they want to know what's going on.'

'She will just worry. Don't tell her.'

I wanted to say I wasn't going to lie to Jane, and try to explain that love was truth, but thought why get into an argument about the definition of love? It seemed counterproductive.

'We always kind of avoid these conversations,' Susie said. 'The obligatory moments, as your father would have said. I was given one hour to get an overnight bag and toothpaste before getting in the ambulance and that has never happened before. I have been such an incredibly organised person. I thought I might never come home. I can't pretend it's not happening now. I got out, anyway. I refused to stay. Better at home than in hospital. I have a wheelchair now. We both do. Stanley's declining much more quickly. He just is incredibly forgetful. And he has been choking so badly and he will not eat small mouthfuls.' She took a breath, not enough of one to allow me to get in a word of sympathy. 'Apart from that I am having a real row with the Brancusse plant nursery in Britain, as the plants they sent were not what I asked for. I wrote and said in your catalogue they are 1.5 m tall and they arrived 75 cm high. They replied with no offer of compensation or change, just some idiotic gardening advice. I said I found their reply flippant, and they should check up on who they were talking to before they told me how to plant a garden.'

'Can't you compromise the design?' I asked.

'I can't. People will run over them or steal them. So I ordered a berberis with a sharp spine. So no one can steal it. Well they can try.'

We finished the conversation. I pictured them both in wheelchairs with Stan losing his mind. It was like *Robot Wars*, with them bashing into each other to get to the drinks trolley, which I remembered was also on wheels.

I phoned her back, and told her I was coming straight out to see them.

I decided to drive. I was fed up with the self-abuse of flying Ryanair. Before I left I received an email from her. It was titled *I have a little list of things for you to bring*.

I braced myself for the word cyanide or strychnine. But no. This is what it said:

English pork sausages. Any flavour. 2 lb.
Pork pie. 2 large ones.
Bacon. 6 packets.
Boned gammon joint × 2.

Oh my god, I thought. She's going to euthanise them with pork products.

TWELVE

Ginster deprivation

I DROVE TO THE FERRY on the last day of March. It was an unusually warm day, and I enjoyed standing on deck, watching the white cliffs of Dover recede while the smokers arced fag butts into the brown English Channel.

I didn't drive South. I motored. I toured. Rather than hammering sleep-deprived, unshaven and bloated with junk food down the motorway, I took small diversions. It was as though a month was scrolled forward in the natural calendar every two hundred miles I travelled. In Paris the leaves were coming out in the street where I stopped for lunch with my friend Nick. I told him the purpose of my mission. He said that his parents, both in their 70s, seeing the end in sight, had embarked on a spending spree. They lived in the suburbs, twenty minutes from the Eiffel Tower, but had put an offer in on a pied-à-terre in town so they could take in shows and not have the trouble of driving home. They had been to Venice for the Anish Kapoor, to New York for the Rauschenburg, and planned a trip to Madrid to spend a couple of days in the Prado.

I meandered to Blois and Chambourg-sur-Indre, with the window open and my foot soft on the pedal. I ate diner in a cafe and overnighted in an auberge on the Loire.

In Poitiers, when I stopped to refuel, I noticed blossom over an orchard beyond the chain-link fence. When I turned off near Toulouse for Susie and Stanley the verges were speckled with yellow cowslips and purple orchids, and the woods had unfolded glossy canopies.

It had grown so warm, hot even, that I took off my jacket and wished I was wearing lighter shoes, when I suddenly remembered the pork. It had been in the back of the car since the night before last when I had bought it in Tesco on Cromwell Road. I also remembered that the two gammon joints, bursting with pigginess through their string vests under the plastic packaging, were reduced in price because they were either on or near to their sell-by date.

The British nosh run was a well-established activity in the expatriate community in the South of France. Since the heightened security measures at airports and Ryanair's desire to get holidaymakers to wear only the clothes they could fit in their pockets, getting unavailable British comestibles in France has grown increasingly difficult. Our people out there were desperate for tea, Marmite, pork pies and bacon, the way the old sailors needed limes to stave off scurvy (though what disease the Brits were keeping at bay with that diet I could only imagine). The greatest delicacy was fresh ham. A boned leg of outdoor-reared English cured ham could cause mayhem. And with Brexit, things were bound to get harder. I could be carrying the last dry-cured bacon across the Channel for months. When I stopped for a cup of coffee near the Dordogne, I drew the roller blind so the contents of my boot were hidden. If a roaming Brit spotted that packaging I could be torn to shreds by a pack of expats, demented from Ginster deprivation. When I got back in the car I thought I smelt something unusual. I feared it might be the pork, which had now been 48 hours in a hot airless boot. At this rate I was going to kill my mum, and possibly a few other expats, with pork. Like a UKIP assassin picking off Europhile traitors. I put my foot down and turned up at Susie's door carrying a straining carrier bag at 11 p.m.

She had got smaller since I last saw her, and her left eye had a reflective glint like a fish scale, I guessed from a growing cataract. Both she and Stanley reminded me of screwed up balls of paper that had been half-flattened. And Susie was crying. I know things are grim when people cry with joy at my arrival. I held her in a hug and felt her bones through the sagging clothes. She was standing as straight as she could but I could see it was hurting her.

'I better put this in the freezer,' I said. She was so unsteady on her feet she moved like she was on board a ferry in a heavy sea, gripping the fridge door for support and then the sideboard, moving her hands before her feet.

'Thank you, thank you. I'm going to be very popular with this,' she said. I am sure she had her strategy well-planned. With that kind of pork you could set the rules in expat France, the way the yanks used nylons to get what they wanted in wartime Britain. Susie would make them listen. She'd invite them round with the promise of Tesco's finest farm-reared rolled shoulder, sit them down and soften them up with an hour of the peace group, before moving onto her garden triumphs. Then, while they were salivating with thoughts of gammon and pineapple, she'd turn the screws with the new car park planting scheme.

The house hadn't gone to pot. But I saw that there were child-gates at the top of the stairs, and I soon worked out why when I saw Stanley piloting his wheel chair after four whiskies. It was not a criminal offence to drive a wheel chair under the influence, but if they ever brought one in, which I expect they will, I don't think Stanley is going to care. He's a drunk wheeler, that's how he rolls.

Susie told me she had had E. coli. 'Apparently they have it in *all* the hospitals in Britain; they don't have it in France at all.' Somehow she got it. But she seemed to be a lot better. I went to bed glad I had driven so many miles to be with them. She *had* been ill. Unlike once or twice in the past when she had faked dying to get

me, and on one occasion my son, over to France ... only
to meet us smiling at the door, saying something like
'you're just in time for a game of boules, then we're going
down to the village for dinner.'

I remember my son's headmaster asking me how my
mother was and having no idea what he was talking
about, although I had told him only two weeks earlier
she was dying.

But they were different this trip. Stanley could only
put one foot about six inches in front of the other and
moved like he had pooed his pants. He was meant to
walk as much as possible but sat all day at his modelling table, retreating into a happy childhood, building
model aeroplanes and ships. His completed models were
displayed not entirely wholeheartedly by my mother in
the house. She permitted a six-foot-long HMS Hood
to lie at anchor in the freezer room downstairs, but was
ambivalent about a magnificent wooden HMS Victory
that hove to in the sitting room under a spotlight,
though the most negative she could get away with was
'the shelf is too big'.

The house possessed the torpor I remembered from
Nanna's care home. Stanley was on the sofa staring at
Cash in the Attic – he wished there was – and he didn't
turn his head when I came in and said hello. Susie was
upstairs asleep. They kept the schedule of Elvis Presley
in his last days. They rose at 11 a.m., slept a lot of the
afternoon, hit the pill bottle and drinks tray at 8 and

shuffled weaving to bed at about 3.30 a.m. Although there were indeed two wheelchairs, my mother did not use hers, and Stanley preferred to stamp in tiny steps like a stroppy toddler. The baby gates were presumably fitted to stop the drinks trolley cannoning off Stanley and down the stairs.

From time to time a nurse called at the house to check up on them. I was in the kitchen when Stanley said 'Ça, c'est mon beau fils.'

The nurse shot me a dark look, as if to say 'Where the hell have you been?' I remembered that we were in a part of rural Catholic France where good offspring look after their parents in their homes, and enjoy the sacrifice.

When she departed, Stanley and I sat down to a bowl of soup. I had noticed that when he ate in front of Susie he made a lot of noise. There was grunting, slurping, sniffing and gurgling on top of the percussive clicking of cutlery on teeth, followed by long choking coughs, which effectively stopped Susie talking, though she tried to raise her voice above the din. Dining just with me he drank his soup in silence, and I thought, that's a thirty year marriage.

He put down his spoon, and asked if he could talk to me off the record. Code for not telling Susie. It was easy to talk in confidence in this house because they both spent so long getting from one room to another that I could hear them coming for hours. I had been using this advantage to avoid them, nipping up the stairs when I heard the clunk of the lift coming into life, or darting onto the balcony when I heard one of them shuffling down the corridor in my direction.

He forgot what he wanted to say, so I said, 'One of the reasons I'm here is that I don't think we should be talking about shortening your lives, but making them as good as possible for as long as they last. What I want to know from you is what you want to do before you die, so I can make it happen, or at least try to. So you are actually doing what you want to do and enjoying life, rather than simply existing.'

'What do I want to do?' he thought, but not for long. 'Me? Marry a rich widow who thinks of sex as much as I do and sail first class with her on the Queen Mary to see my American descendants in New York. And I want a full-time carer, to dress and bathe me, she's called Maria, she worked for a friend, a very intelligent young girl. With lovely hands and slim body so she doesn't take up too much space, though her breasts are large. So surprising really with a waist that slim ...'

'I'll put that on the list,' I said. 'Is there anything else you want to do, with Mummy for instance?'

'Oh. You mean before *she* dies?' He sunk into silence. I guessed he was running through the score of things he wanted to do, striking each one out, trying to find one he might conceivably be permitted to do. 'My model making,' he said, back in little boy mode, pointing to the scale model of the Sopwith Camel he had recently ordered on the Internet.

'Well we'll put that on the list. Time for hobbies. Very important,' I said. 'But we must think of more things. I am going to do the same thing with Susie. Ask her what she wants to do before she dies. It's important.'

'I can tell you. She wants to rule the world,' he said, then held up his finger. 'I have just remembered what I wanted to talk to you about. Money.' He rambled around the subject for a bit and then came to the point: he wanted to know if I'd pony up for Susie's care. 'A full-time carer, living in,' he explained, 'which is what she will need, is six hundred francs, I mean euros a week. That's near enough thirty thousand pounds a year. We need you to pay for that.' He smiled at me, his take-pity-on-me-I'm-just-an-old-man-with-slow-onset-dementia smile. Quite a useful weapon to have in the arsenal. I thought, let's get back to assisted suicide. I had seriously underestimated its benefits.

THIRTEEN

A bowl full of wishes

I T WAS HARDER TO get Susie to talk about the future. She had a clever way of veering off towards the car park planting scheme. We sat at the kitchen table because she could not get up easily from the sofas. I had suggested the day before that she might think of replacing them with something with higher seats, but she had dismissed this as idiocy.

'Why?' I said. 'You can't sit in your sitting room. *That* seems silly. Why not get an armchair?'

'The look,' she said. 'I conceived of this design and I will not have it spoiled.'

'I understand,' I said. 'Your time is limited,' I soldiered on. 'So rather than talking about shortening it, I think we should look at ways of improving it, and making it enjoyable. So let's make a list of the things that are really important to you, not to anyone else, and let's see if we can make them happen.'

'Is this what you were doing with Stanley?'

'Yes.'

'What did he say?'

'We hardly got started.'

'Did I tell you, he hasn't shown me his will, so naturally I have not shown him mine,' she said, to strike back.

'Where shall we start?'

The Americans call it a bucket list, but I didn't like the term. Buckets are for slops, shit, leaks and KFC. I was thinking more of a trug list. Or a rose bowl full of wishes.

'Is there maybe somewhere you wanted to go? Stanley mentioned New York.'

'Who with?'

'Some friends and family …'

'What friends?'

'I don't know if you know them.'

'We only have mutual friends,' she said and I felt a stab of pain for poor old Stanley.

'Maybe you would like to go somewhere?'

But she wasn't going to be lured so easily into my plan. I was not sure why. Maybe because it removed from her the comfort that her suicide plan was giving her.

'I gave Katie 400 quid for her gap-year trip to India on condition she didn't go to Goa and waste her time with hippies.'

Katie was Susie's 19-year-old granddaughter. I said nothing, hoping Katie was lying stoned on the beach in Goa writing postcards to Susie saying how wonderful the Malabar Caves are.

'I suppose we could go on a cruise. But what about embarkation and disembarkation?' She was right, I wouldn't like to see her and Stan tackle a swaying gangplank in a heavy swell. 'Of course we've been everywhere. South America. Stunning architecture. We saw *everything*. You see we were there for three weeks.'

She told me she had talked to Stanley about a Norwegian cruise where the passengers didn't go ashore. They could admire the fjords and icebergs while sitting on deck.

'That sounds a possibility,' I said. 'I'll write that down.'

'Would you like to make a vinaigrette?' Susie asked.

I said yes, put down my pen, went to the kitchen and opened the cupboard.

'That's the oil, there,' she said from behind me.

I said nothing as I unscrewed the top. When I reached for the vinegar I heard an intake of breath. 'Not too sharp.'

I put down the vinegar. 'Why don't you make it?' I said, seething. And I thought – I am going mad. Calm down. She's an old lady.

Then came the matter of the peppers.

Stanley had said that he wanted to cook dinner one night, and carefully picked a dish from an old schoolbook of recipes: quenelles in a saffron sauce. We looked through the fridge and discovered that all the ingredients were there, excepting green and yellow peppers. I said that I would act as Stanley's sous chef, and start by going to buy the peppers.

I was mooching around the house around lunch-time when Susie said 'Oh – that's a pity, you've missed the shop.'

'What do you mean?' I said.

'The local shop and all the supermarkets close at midday on Sunday.'

'The supermarkets too?'

'Yes,' she said. And this is why I thought I was going mad: she looked like she was happy to tell me, and – in addition – she had watched me for an hour doing nothing and could have mentioned that the shops closed at midday before one minute past 12. Stanley did an excellent impression of a little boy who had lost his ball.

I said 'Oh well, I'll go and buy the peppers tomorrow and we shall eat quenelles in saffron sauce tomorrow night.'

Susie lurched sideways, grabbed at the counter and grappled her way to the fridge. 'I think I'll have a glass of bubbly,' she said.

The next morning I drove to the local shop. Predictably, it was closed. It was as though the nice Syrian man who ran it waited for my car to pull up in the car park and quickly flicked the sign and turned off the lights. I drove to another village and found a small grocery. I parked the car, walked in and there between me and the well-coiffed female shopkeeper was a box of yellow peppers.

'Bonjour, ca va?' I said.

'Ca va,' she said.

'Vous etes ouvert,' I smiled.

'Non,' she said.

'Is it possible …,' I started in French, pointing to the peppers.

'I open tomorrow at eleven,' she said, brushing past me to wheel the carousel of postcards from under the awning. She held the door open for me to leave.

Napoleon had said that the English were a nation of shopkeepers. He failed to add that the French were most definitely not. Supermarkets aside, the silliness of French shops was quite extraordinary.

Had I been permitted to buy a pepper, it would not have surprised me if she had said 'Bon choix, monsieur. Parfait. It is a gift? Of course! Eh bien.' She would then have found a shiny box which she would place the pepper in before tying a bow on it and making it curl with a pull of the scissors, all the while complimenting me on my clever idea of giving someone a vegetable for their special day. Behind me a queue would have formed, eager to have a look and pass judgement on my choice of gift and the wrapping. 'Mignon!' they would squeak approvingly.

There are other ways the French have of making a simple transaction unnecessarily complex. In this version I would arrive at the shop, ask for a pepper and after some whispered conversation into a phone, a door would open at the back of the shop and a neat little Frenchman would appear, shake my hand and conduct me into his clutter-free office with two futuristic moulded plastic chairs and a glass desk.

'I understand you wish to buy a pepper. Oui?'

'Yes please.'

He would unfold a glossy pamphlet covered in badly posed photographs and garish upbeat graphics.

'We no longer sell single yellow peppers. That was the old days. We are phazing them out. France is a totally modern country now. In a year, it will be illegal to cook with an old farm-grown pepper. It is part of the Macron revolution. Now we have a new design, produced entirely without any contact with the soil or sunshine. C'est marvelleux. These peppers are actually grown in their packaging, and are picked fully encased in plastic for maximum hygiene and convenience. I have here a contract that guarantees you access to these new peppers through my franchise. Simply provide me with your bank details, passport, carte de sejour, driving licence, marriage certificate and three utility bills and it will be my pleasure to sign you up for our introductory offer of 6000 euros for a ten year contract. The peppers come fully guaranteed and for peace of mind a service engineer is on call for only 80 euros an hour to ensure you have the appropriate gas fittings in your kitchen. The inspections take place every ten days and are obligatory. Then you will be fully compliant with the new pepper regulations.'

So I drove to Leclerc, where I danced around the supermarket as if I had just finished a ten-year jail sentence. I bought the peppers. Back at base, Susie had already started cooking dinner, so we agreed to postpone Stanley's fish dish until the next evening. Stanley stuck out his lower lip but I reassured him that tomorrow it would actually happen. I gathered that he had basically been banned from cooking by Susie on some grounds or other, and to be frank he was a bit of an accident waiting to happen around an electric hob and sharp knives. The next day I came downstairs and saw Susie bent over the cooker trying to lift a hot pan.

'Let me do that,' I said.

'Thank you,' said she. 'It's soup. For lunch. Tomato … and pepper.'

'You didn't use Stanley's peppers did you?'

'Oh! I forgot they were for him.'

Stanley shuffled in, in his tiny steps. We broke the news. He nearly cried. I nearly screamed. And I thought, am I imagining this, or is she really trying to sabotage his goddam quenelles and saffron sauce? We ate artichokes after the soup. Susie said 'I am the only person who knows how to eat an artichoke properly.'

I thought: *You are the* only *person who would say that.* To be competitive about eating. Then I reprimanded myself for being so uncharitable. I was thinking like the worst kind of care-home employee. I had become impatient, bitchy and harsh. I was meant to be making things better for Susie and Stanley.

I decided I needed a break to get back on track.

FOURTEEN

Red lines

I HAD BEEN AWAY FOR a couple of days when I descended the snaky mountain road, the wheel slipping through my palms, and accelerated north along roads striped with plane tree shadows. Ahead I started to see the cute hilltop villages of the Tarn rising from the spooky French monocultural farmland. Back at Susie and Stanley's I unpacked, went downstairs and asked my mother if we could all have a talk.

'What about?' she said.

'About what we talked about last time I was here, you know, the suicide thing ...' I said.

'Listen to this,' she said. Some classical music blasted from the dusty speaker.

'Berlioz,' she shouted over it.

I sat down and watched her close her eyes, put her head to one side and smile.

'His requiem!' she called to me. 'So triumphant!'

I could see that she wasn't going to turn it down, so I looked at the track listing and saw it was 27 minutes long. I turned it down.

'Do you want that played at your funeral? I was thinking that one of the things we should think about in this whole operation is what kind of funeral you want.'

'I don't want a fuss,' she said. 'Cremate me and spread me on the new planting in the car park. It's all in my letter of wishes with the lawyer. Did I tell you about *mon petit triomph* against the mayor about the watering of the new planting?' she flashed a smile. 'Of course the French have absolutely no idea about gardening. No idea. But I am charging them for that hosepipe. And the water. They don't know it yet, but the Commune will pay.'

I stood my ground under the barrage, and when she realised she was cornered I turned off the music and sat with her on the sofa. The weather was warm, the terrace door open, and shafts of red sun fell deep in the room.

Stanley was in the next room absorbed in a scale model of a back hoe digger he'd got for his birthday. I called him but it was useless, so I jumped up and asked him to come through. He followed in his little boy footsteps.

'What's this about?' he asked.

'It's about the subject we have been talking about a lot together,' Susie said.

'Sex!' Stanley exclaimed, delighted.

'No. The other one,' she said.

Stanley looked confused.

'I wanted to talk about the idea Mummy said you and she had discussed, of ending your lives together,' I said.

Stanley's brow wrinkled. 'But what if I am in the middle of a model aeroplane?' he said. 'My new Sopwith Camel has a thousand pieces. It could take a year.' He looked like his toy was about to be taken away. But we were actually talking about his life.

'What are you saying?' I asked quietly.

'I can't in all honesty see myself doing it now,' Stanley said.

I felt Susie twitch beside me.

'That's not what you said to me,' she said. 'You are saying something different.'

'That's all right, Mummy,' I said. I couldn't believe what I was hearing. Even by her standards this was extreme.

I asked Stanley 'Is this what you want to say? That you are *not* thinking about suicide?'

'Yes,' said Stanley. 'Anyway, what if one of us took it and not the other?' he mimed not taking a pill at the last moment and pointed at Susie.

He's going to pay for that, I thought.

'What about the idea we had of dying holding hands on the bed?' she asked.

'But I'm not in pain or ill,' he said.

I swallowed.

'That's not what we agreed together,' Susie said.

'But it is now,' said Stanley. 'In all honesty I cannot see myself wanting to die.'

Susie looked deflated, beaten.

I thought how mentally competent Stanley was, and how he hammered up memory and hearing loss when he wanted to escape the demands of Susie and the world generally. My mother looked miserable. Her old bent body sagged beside me. I looked across at her baggy face, caught by rather cruel light. I smiled at her. God knows why. She had a minute earlier been trying to tell her husband that he was morally obliged to kill himself on a date of her choosing.

'Would it still be something you would consider doing on your own?' I asked. 'It looks as though it's unlikely that both of you will reach the same point at same time.'

She nodded. I thought I could hear her saying to herself, I should never have let Guy get Stanley in the meeting.

A minute later the resignation seemed to set in. She looked so small and so scared. She was going to have to do it without Stanley. He was indeed looking supremely well. He had told me that his hair was actually turning from white to grey. Stanley wasn't losing his mind or falling apart. She was the one in so much pain – she took enough tramadol every six hours to flatten me for a week. She was going to have to go on ahead.

'I would do it,' she said, 'when the time comes.'

She could hardly back out now, I thought, and then the idea struck me that she was now going to have to kill herself to prove to us that she wasn't just trying to kill Stanley.

'When would you think you might get to the point …?' I asked.

'When I am bedbound and can't look after myself. You know. Go to the lavatory on my own. Things like that.'

Her red line was wiping her own bum. Fair enough, I thought.

In an act of solidarity Stanley said 'I wouldn't mind having the means to hand, if they were ever needed. A bottle of whisky and some pills,' though he added, 'but only to be used if I want to.'

Susie nodded.

She was going to have to go it alone. She wasn't going to hold onto Stanley's hand on the bed. She had to do it empty-handed. That's death, I guess. It's not a group activity, unless there's something very wrong. Here was one thing she wasn't able to control.

As this was sinking in, I watched on Susie's face and in her twitching hands the unusual sight of fear. I put my arm around her. I felt love for her, but I also felt another more surprising emotion. That emotion was admiration. I was proud of her. She was a woman of principle, a woman of substance. She was going to walk the walk, and not just talk it. She had a red line. She had declared that there was a level beneath which her life was no longer worth living. And she meant what she said.

FIFTEEN

The unsanctified burial ground

A NY IMMEDIATE ACTION FROM Susie was, I thought, unlikely as she had invited her grand-children and great-grandchildren out for a holiday a month hence, in August; I doubted she would kill her-self before then. Unless of course she was planning for them to come not for a vacation but for her funeral, which with all the accommodation and flights booked would be churlish to miss. It would certainly ensure a well-attended service, which would look impressive to her French friends. But I doubted this was the strategy. I had already seen Susie preparing menus and meal plans, so I thought it safe to nip back to Britain to attend to some business, though I couldn't get her situation out of my mind and talked about it to anyone who didn't know her and would be unlikely ever to meet her.

Extraordinarily, I found that virtually everyone I brought the subject up with had a relative or friend who was either contemplating killing themselves, or had actually done it. Johnno, the carpenter fitting windows in my barn, had a mum who had killed herself, quite deliberately, with whisky. Ian, the electrician, said an old man whose immersion heater he had fixed recently had gone out in his pyjamas on a cold night to feed his llamas and die. William, the record producer I sat opposite to on a plane had accompanied his aunt to Dignitas. My friend Nicky's mother threw herself out of her bedroom window, though she had forgotten she had been moved from her country house into a bungalow, and had just got a bit muddy and scratched by the cotoneaster. Her first words upon being rescued were 'I'm so sorry. My parachute can't have opened properly.' And at a lunch party I attended under the Tor at Glastonbury, of eight people present, three of us were involved with the same activity.

One had an aunt with Parkinson's who had lost her voice, was bedbound and thought it was time to go, but the other had a story more chilling.

'Sarah Seymour got the doctor to do it,' a sexy 70-year-old woman with thick white hair and a twinkle in her eyes said. 'She had cancer but didn't do anything about it. You know what she was like …' The other guests nodded. 'He prescribed her the drugs and told her to take them all at one time. She got Jeremy and Joshua there, and her sister too, and went upstairs while they were all in the house, and died in her sleep.'

Everyone said 'Ahh,' sympathetically.

'She was a great a fan of your books Guy,' the woman continued. 'She turned us all on to *One People*. She was always talking about it.'

And she decided to bring her life to a dignified close. A hard-core fan, who had spread the word among the unconverted. Couldn't she have gone into a hospice and stretched it out for a few months so she could talk about the brilliance of my novels while tenderly holding the hands of nurses and distant relatives? Oh no. She had to kill herself, with no care at all for my book sales.

Despite the huge number of people apparently plotting with friends and family to do away with themselves, the official figures I found online seemed to say that very few of them actually did it. And the number was in decline, whereas from the talk around the dinner tables and in the pubs I frequented, you would expect it to be increasing. In the 1930s, 50 in every 100,000 people over 65 ended their own lives. Now it was a mere 37. It's men around 35 who are saying they've had enough. But a young man killing himself is not the subject of this book.

When I dug deeper into the unsanctified burial ground of old suicide statistics, I found a report that reviewed the figures between 1963 and 2009 and drew the general conclusion that officially recorded suicides were only about a third of the true number. I learnt that the old canard that Sweden has a high suicide rate was almost certainly due to their more accurate reporting of the event. Many countries have ceased defending the reliability of their suicide numbers. All of this also goes under-reported, like the suicides themselves, the whole subject not lost in the long grass but deliberately fly-tipped into a gully.

One of the principal problems was that two very different activities, viz. deciding the time and manner of your death at the end of a life, and cutting short a life half-way through, shared the same word: suicide. This was akin to classifying surgery under knife crime.

But even non-geriatric suicide has not always had such a bad reputation. In Roman times, those citizens who wanted to kill themselves merely applied to the Senate, and if their reasons were judged sound, they were then given hemlock on the house. It was specifically forbidden in three cases: those accused of capital crimes, soldiers and slaves – because it was *uneconomic* for the latter two to die. Not an argument you could use on old people hoovering up scarce NHS resources.

It was that beacon of kindness and sensitivity the medieval Roman Catholic Church that decreed suicide should be punished in all cases. In France, the dead person's body was drawn through the streets, face down, and then hung or thrown on a garbage heap. Elsewhere, suicides were excommunicated and buried alone, on the outskirts of the city, without a headstone or marker and never in consecrated ground. Additionally, all of the person's property was confiscated. I wondered whether by chance it was forfeited to the Church.

The secularisation of society questioned attitudes. David Hume denied suicide was a crime as it affected no one and was potentially to the advantage of the individual. In his 1777 *Essays on Suicide and the Immortality of the Soul* he wrote: "Why should I prolong a miserable existence, because of some frivolous advantage which the public may perhaps receive from me?"

In 1786 *The Times* initiated a spirited debate on the motion "Is suicide an act of courage?" In 1832 The Burial of Suicides Act abolished the legal requirement in England of burying suicides at crossroads. In 1882 the deceased were permitted daylight burial in England, and by the mid-20th century, suicide ceased to be a criminal offence with the passing of the Suicide Act, which received Royal assent on the 3 August 1961; the same Act made it an offence to assist in a suicide. When I was reading the Act, the penalty for being caught assisting a suicide leapt out at me: a maximum term of 14 years in jail. I wondered whether anyone had actually done the stretch that I was looking at, and was alarmed to discover that two had, though in neither of those cases was the person planning to die old. Assisted suicide is now legal in Germany and Sweden, though the person has to administer the act themselves. Lone suicide is now legal in much of the Western world, though the stain poured over it by the Church has still not been washed out.

Martin Amis, who by his own admission writes a great deal about and around suicide, calls it 'the most somber of all subjects – the saddest story.' He says that the writer is the antithesis of the suicide by 'constantly applauding and creating life.' He goes on to say 'suicide is omnicide ... The murderer kills just one person. The suicide kills everybody.'

He is wrong. For a start, murderers often kill more than one person, metaphorically and literally. And suicide does not always kill everybody. Very often, with the interminable geriatric care we now have, it releases. Diana Athill, at 100, wryly said this morning on Radio 4 'at my age, life is somewhat overrated and people make too much of a thing about death.'

I heard of an elderly woman who on being told by her doctor she had a year to live replied 'A year? I only want 4 months.' She reminded me of a group of upbeat American seniors I had been shown on the web who had not only formed a club to help each other design and build their own coffin but had made a musical about it.

Amanda's granny was being kept alive by the Nottingham care home, if by the definition of being alive you mean breathing, eating and blinking. She barely recognised Amanda but confidently identified Amanda's son Haruka as his uncle, Mike. She could not in any manner look after herself, but was still strong and looked like lasting a good few years.

We really need a second word or phrase to describe what Susie and her fellow travellers were contemplating. And it requires a nomenclature that evokes the reasonableness – and even wisdom – of those who did it.

SIXTEEN

Criminal sentences

T HE SUBJECT OF KILLING yourself by choice in old age is taboo. It doesn't even have a name, so it's almost impossible to talk about. We are scared of it, we are banned from doing it, we are discouraged from knowing about it. They criminalise even writing about it. Here is an unlawful sentence: I am going to help my mother finish her life in the way she wants. There aren't many criminal sentences. It's good to write a literal rather than metaphorical one for a change. Maybe I will be prosecuted for typing those words and if I am I will relish the opportunity to argue their legitimacy in front of a judge.

One of the reasons people misreport healthy Self-Deletion (I am clearly failing to find a good phrase) is because it affects insurance payouts. The life insurance companies, those bountiful fonts of humanity and benevolence, don't pony up after a Closure. (Closure is also no good, with its echoes of bankruptcy and failure). They too are part of the conspiracy to make you limp every last agonising yard of your life no matter how crippled you are, how ugly the scenery.

The good news – it seems – is that many more people are taking control of their own destinies than the authorities realise. Naturally there are groups on the Internet raising awareness. Dignity in Dying 'A heartbeat is not the only sign of life' is the one I spent most time perusing, and was where I discovered the celebrities endorsing the cause: Ian McEwen, Sir Patrick Stewart and Jo Brand. Not bad ambassadors. McEwen wrote: *The issue is not really of death but of how you live out the last chapter, those last sentences.*

The difficulties faced by advocates of Conscious Dying are similar to those who support Abortion. I am pro-choice at both ends of life, and proud to say it. But it's a hard sell when opponents make them both an issue of murder rather than human rights.

I spoke to a Tory ex-minister, now in the House of Lords, who had made a speech in the House when Rob Marris' Private Member's Bill on assisted suicide was overwhelmingly voted down in 2015. We met in Yorkshire, where he lived, after I had toured the ruins of Jervaulx Abbey, thinking I might make a comparison between them and Stanley's mind. We talked over a glass of good wine in a rose-scented garden. He was, at 87, portly and a bit slow physically but smiling and as sharp as a rose thorn. He told me with pride that he had opposed Marris' Bill.

'Why?' I asked.

'For the simple reason that it was an invitation to unscrupulous people to kill wealthy relatives.'

'But don't the rights of those who want to choose how and when they die come into it?'

'They cannot outweigh the rights of those who we endanger.' He went on to say that reformers said they only wanted assisted suicide to be available for the terminally ill, but then by incremental extension more people would be included. He spoke as if people generally wanted to kill their relatives. But all evidence pointed in exactly the opposite direction. It would have meant more to me if he had taken the line that the taking of a life – or the abetting in the taking of a life – was *in principle* wrong. But his pragmatic line, though one I had heard many times, and which was taken by more than just this peer during the debate in Parliament, seemed bizarre. This was the narrative that the newspapers and newsfeeds loved to push. Here is a headline I recently read: *Pharmacist murdered his father with lethal fruit smoothie then said it was assisted suicide, court heard.* My first thought was *You wouldn't get a fruit smoothie down Stanley.* But my second was, why should they want to discredit courageous and bold citizens who are helping people choose the place, time and manner of their own death? The headline we should be reading is *Thousands of patients kept in captivity and tortured by the NHS.*

People do not want to murder their relatives. It is incredibly rare. Murder, in the UK, is an extraordinary event, except on TV and in films, where for some silly reason it's commonplace. The figures are clear: in

Britain we don't want to kill people. Out of a population of 56 million, 310 men and 180 women were killed in 2015. Half of the women were killed by their partners. Only 15 per cent were killed by other members of their family, i.e. not their partners. That is 46 males, and 27 females. And that included children. We don't know how many of those were elderly, because, surprise surprise, the government is not collecting homicide figures for the over 80s. But even if they were all geriatrics, which they were not, it shows that there is no great desire to knock off an inconvenient granny or grandad. It doesn't even happen on TV and in films. In a decidedly unscientific survey I kept count of the number of murders I saw on TV over about a month of viewing. It was well over 500, including zombies, out of an estimated general population in the dramas of about 2000. It's dangerous being in movies or TV serials. But even in this land of carnage I didn't see ONE family knocking off an inconvenient geriatric relative. It is a rubbish argument to say the law on assisted dying is to protect public safety.

I dropped the subject with the ex-minister. He wasn't going to change his mind, he had said all there was for him to say on the matter and I was drinking his wine in his garden (or his son's to be accurate). But I definitely felt as though I were being accused of accessory to murder by advancing the case for helping my mum kill herself when she wanted.

On all the many occasions I had discussed the subject of Signing Off with relatives of the person contemplating it I never had the slightest doubt that they were doing it entirely in the interests of the person who, exhausted and agonised by life, wished to end their life. It is that obdurate threesome the state, the Church and the medical profession that has fostered the notion that families want to kill their aged relatives only for malicious or pecuniary reasons. The design of the syringe driver used in hospitals on geriatrics for pain relief has been modified recently to prevent the midazolam being plunged too quickly. This new design is predicated on the idea that relatives, gathered around an elderly patient's bedside are homicidal maniacs. They are not. We are not, I should say. There is a thick black line between murdering someone and helping them choose the time and manner of their departure. But no one is allowed openly to acknowledge this or talk about it without being accused – by politicians, doctors or clergymen – of being a killer.

The medical profession seems to delight in using the Hippocratic oath to torture the aged and their families, but a GP I spoke to did point out to me that it was unfair that the doctors were being picked on to do this onerous job, which they hadn't signed up for, and it was a fair point. The doctors really should not have to shoulder the responsibilities of checking out their patients. Preventing all suicide is a stated target of the

World Health Organization. The doctors, priests and politicians are like reverse bouncers at the door of the party which is life. Their job is stop guests leaving. To stop them going to meet the old man by the lake when they want. What does that say about the party? If you want to leave, it's usually a sign you are not enjoying it. Keeping everyone trapped in life prevents the question of who actually wants to be there unasked and definitely unanswered. Those who kill themselves are clearly saying it's not much cop any more. Doctors, politicians and clerics take this as a personal affront, a criticism of geriatric care, society and the efficacy of religious belief. But it is not a criticism of hospitals or doctors or priests. It's a criticism of old age. It's an acknowledgement of the rock-hard facts of getting to the end of life and the human body and mind falling apart. Can we not admit that? It's like scrapping a car rather than having it break down every time we try to use it. Things die. This is nature. Accept it. And learn to do it with dignity and even beauty.

It is as mad to legislate against leaving life as it would be to make a law that requires a human to have permission to enter it. But it takes a lot of guts to kill yourself when the time is right, and not many of us are up to the challenge. (It shocked me that despite so many people talking about Dignitas, only 273 people from the UK had used its service in the 16 years up to 2014.) Ernest Hemingway was up to the job of Signing Off. He felt his considerable powers, both intellectual and physical, failing, and he knew what lay ahead. He had completed *A Moveable Feast* – an exquisite memoir of being a young man in Paris, both deeply romantic and rigorously unsentimental. And when has an American before or since written about Paris without trowelling on the cheese? A year later he was being described by his editor, Aaron Hotchner, as 'unusually hesitant, disorganised and confused and suffering from failing eyesight ... constantly worried about money and safety.' Hemingway was sent to the Mayo Clinic and given electroconvulsive therapy only to be 'released in ruins.' A few days later, on the morning of 2 July 1961 he shot himself with his favourite gun.

His family released a statement saying it was an accident, which they later amended. To me, it was the great writer's final triumph. He had a line below which he would not live. Life was for riding, not clinging onto in desperation. Hemingway had seen a life of action, of love, and of towering artistic achievement, and he had decided he wasn't going to slide into dribbling infancy. And good luck to him. There was, it is true, a lot of suicide in his family: his brother and his father had also killed themselves. But at no point in his life before the end did Hemingway attempt or contemplate suicide, as far as we know. It was a brave and logical move, not an act of mental illness, as I believe most pre-geriatric suicides to be. Hemingway had a red line. I don't know what it was. A writer once told me that

Hemingway had been asked to write the funeral oration for John F. Kennedy by his widow Jackie, and had been unable to do it. I had pictured Hemingway staring at his portable typewriter, frozen with the realisation that he could no longer get the words onto the page without parodying himself. He had grimly accepted that he had lost it. Asked by the nation to eulogise the young slain president, the greatest living author found himself lost for words, unequal to the task, unable to make sense of the killing for millions of grieving countrymen. To some it would have been a moment of rueful reflection, and an announcement to any who cared that it was time for retirement. But not Hemingway. Not Papa. He didn't possess a white flag, much less run one up the pole. He was a man of honour and he took the honourable course ... When I checked this story I discovered it was nonsense, as John F. Kennedy was assassinated on 22 November 1963, two years and four months *after* Hemingway was buried under a simple and elegant headstone on his Idaho estate. The reason he didn't write the funeral oration was because he had been stone dead for 28 months, which was as sound an excuse for not turning in copy as I have ever heard.

Whatever it was, the great American author had his red line. The thing about these lines, as far as I can see, is that if they are a long way ahead, they seem sharply defined. My mother's was going to the lavatory unaided. What could be more simple? But when you got closer they blurred. You hurt your hand, which was expected to heal in a couple of days, but during that time you couldn't wipe your bottom. Hold on. There's the line. But it didn't quite count. Indeed, in three days, the hand is well enough to go to the loo on your own, and you probably smile as you wipe your bottom saying I'm actually quite glad I didn't top myself. And the next time you can't do it, lying in bed on a drip, or with a broken pelvis from dissolving bones, you say to yourself 'Well, I've had this done to me before and it's really not that bad.'

What was my own red line? Because I definitely required one. I refuse to slide into infantilised catatonia. I know exactly where mine is: when an unrecognisable woman – or man – comes into my room and says *Hello Dad.* When I don't know who my own children are … at that moment I will green light PROJECT TOP GUY. And I will be disciplined. When I start arguing to myself that it was just the light, or she's got a new hairstyle, or he's wearing a new shirt, or that I always have trouble with names, I will issue a stern reprimand to myself. Guy! I shall shout. If I can remember my name, that is. And therein lies the problem. If I can't identify the two people I most love in the world, will I be able to have the wherewithal to knock myself off the perch? Planning will be required.

And that is what Susie was engaged in.

SEVENTEEN

Tim Berners me

SUSIE AND STANLEY HAD been using the Internet for five or six years, but had apparently never stumbled across Google. My mother's use of the computer was eccentric. She didn't know how to copy and paste, or about the backwards arrow. Every web page she went onto she carefully typed into the browser, using even the www., and for a while attempted to print out each page in case she couldn't find it again, on her psychologically damaged printer, which either withdrew into sullen non co-operation, or babbled nonsense. Luckily she gave up with the printer.

It was quite fun teaching her to use the tools, and she made me feel like I was Tim Berners Lee. She believed that only *I* knew about Google.

I told her there was an easier way to find old pages than look at the list she had written down in her notebook, and advised her to go into her HISTORY and right click. She looked confused. I drew up a chair and sat next to her. My knees pushed up against the dusty whirring box under her desk. The screen was so dim and indistinct it took me a long time to find the arrow which she was zigzaggging across the screen.

'Go to History,' I said, 'and right click.'

'What's right click?' she asked. Six years she had been using this computer and mouse.

I reached for the mouse and right clicked.

'How did you do that?'

'I pressed this,' I said, showing her.

'What?'

'Put your hand on the mouse,' I said.

I put my hand over hers. Her skin was so soft, the bones so defined. The rings I had known all my life looked so bulky on her withered digits. I put my index finger on hers and nudged it across to the button, and pressed.

'Oh! That's how you get that!'

'And with this wheel we scroll down to TODAY, and you can see the pages you have been on, and if you left click, like this, it comes back up.'

'Oh! I did that once before and wondered how you did that. You are clever.'

'And this takes you back to Google.'

'What exactly is Google?' she asked.

'It takes you to the pages you need to go to.'

'How?'

'Well. What's a question we want to ask? Any question.'

After a short deliberation she said 'How much water does a berberis need?'

I typed the words in and told her to press ENTER. Pleasingly the first web page read:

WATERING BERBERIS, INSTRUCTIONS AND TIPS.

She read it in silence, then looked at me and smiled.

'You are clever. Show Stanley.'

A couple of days later I was downstairs researching how many old people killed themselves. I scrolled down the history to look for a site I had seen earlier and I saw that Susie had been looking at overdose information pages. The drug tramadol leapt out at me – I knew she had been trying to buy it on the Internet.

She *was* going to do it. She was resolved. It was just a question of when. We were moving into the endgame. I decided to ask her exactly what role she needed me to play in the denouement, and make sure funeral plans were agreed. At first I felt shock that we were finally on the home stretch. Then I was pleased. This book needed a death.

EIGHTEEN

Enter Jeeves

IN THE TARN, I RENTED a studio apartment a couple of cobbled alleys away from Susie and Stanley, to watch – and if necessary take part – in the final act. I became familiar with the sounds of my place: the creak of the staircase, a mournful tolling bell at dawn, the hiss of my neighbour's pressure cooker, and, most delightful, the piano notes from someone, I never saw who, learning to play Scott Joplin's *Ragtime* in a room with open shutters above an arch. Tentative at first, she – I pictured a girl of about 11 – grew more fluent. On Thursday afternoons the piece was played right through without a mistake. I guessed that that was the piano teacher. Then the next day it was played over and over with mistakes in it, though fewer each time. At the end of the month it became 'Für Elise'.

As the weather grew hot in June, I left my front door open and my neighbour's collie Zorro would barge in, sniff around my desk and ask me what I was up to before wandering home. I made the first sightings in and around the village of the British Tourist trudging up the street past my window. In rural France we have our own species, quite different to the Beach and Spanish varieties. Identifiable by areas of mottled pale flesh on thighs and upper arms, the result of over-wintering in the home counties, and touching attempts to seem French. A family toiled past my house. Mum wore a bulgy Breton fisherman's jersey and had a Provençal basket on her arm. I wondered whether in some cute Cotswold village there was a French family on holiday getting into the local culture, garbed in wife-beaters, carrying six-packs of Stella and looking for a kebab shop. As the Brits passed my window on their way to the medieval square, Dad slipped his hand under mum's arm but she shrugged him off and he fell behind. Dad's shorts had the look of a garment bought by a wife. There was going to be no flirting in that pleated navy blue pair with the bright white drawstring. The kids slouched along beside him, fighting – so different to the little French automatons who all chatted gaily with their parents and treated each other with eerie respect. When I was walking over to the care home for a shift, I saw holiday Dad on his own talking into his phone.

'I'm afraid I am in le maison du chien, a ce moment,' he said, and chuckled. He put the phone away and approached the café, looking anxious, about to be linguistically exposed by a menu. He'd struggle to keep the waiter from switching into bad English, which made it feel less like a holiday.

I found Susie waking from a nap on the sofa, and asked her if she had decided to go ahead.

She answered 'Absolutely, yes. And I have decided to use tramadol. I read a case study on the Internet of a boy who took between 40 and 60. I was going to ask the doctor to prescribe some regularly and stash some away each month, but I have realised that that could implicate her in some way, which I don't want to do because she has looked after me and Stanley so well, so I'm going to buy them off the Internet. There's a company in India who will send them in packs of ten. Isn't that helpful?'

A few days later I sat near the British family outside Le Bar des Arcades. Georges, who ran the café, was not someone I would imagine being drawn to work in tourism. He did not exude bonhomie so much as extinguish it. I was told he did smile, but the last time was four years ago, when a tourist scraped his hire car down a wall. George could serve a coffee like a writ for bankruptcy. But even he had partially dropped his look of open contempt, and the anglos were definitely relaxed. Dad had the hint of a suntan, the kids were happily exhausted from swimming, the *gite* was working out now they'd moved the furniture around, and when dad put his hand on mum's pink arm she smiled at him. The local expats sat hunched up at the other end of the bar, smoking rollies, waiting to pick their kids up from school and muttering about going back to Britain.

There was no work, as far as I could see, not only for the expats, but for virtually anyone. Through a carefully thought-out programme the French government had forced the young to leave the village, move to the city and work for corporations, where they were both protected and enmeshed for life in health and housing benefits they could never afford to walk away from. The few who remained in the village were effectively banned from working. Any person trying to give them work was warned off with red tape and taxes. British people didn't dare to pay cash for a small odd-job in case they were informed on by neighbours and marched off to the authorities, either to be shot or, worse, registered as an employer. If a chippy came in to fix a shelf, it obliged you, as his employer, to pretty well look after him for the rest of his life, including supplying health insurance, paternity leave and a full index-linked pension until his death. It was a very good way of killing the economy in Castelnau, and sapped all entrepreneurial spirit. There was not, for instance, a single available taxi in the community when I was there.

There was only one man going to give out work in the village and that was the mayor. He used the patronage wisely, employing mainly middle-aged French men, also known as his mates, to work on various follies around the place. Projects included the installation of benches with poetry written on them, and the renovation of the tourist information office – a place I had never seen a visitor enter – including a hand-cut stone wheelchair ramp and wrought iron railings.

No expense was spared on the mayorial schemes. One I grew familiar with, as I watched it for weeks from where I worked at my desk, was the resurfacing of a car park. Not my mother's car park. In any other town in any other country, this car park, behind her house, would have been considered perfectly serviceable for another decade. But the mayor had his mates to give work to, and with this project he could get a lot of them involved. He had decided to change the railings, which had nothing wrong with them: a project that would involve a rail designer, a handrail engineer, a barrier surveyor, and numerous specialist rail erection consultants, all the kind of people who abound in France. A year later, the railings were still a work in progress. But the resurfacing of the car park, which was about the size of two tennis courts, was done ridiculously quickly, in just four months. In most places it would have taken four men two days.

The job involved, I counted, seven men. First came silver-haired executives in suits and expensive cars who eyed up the project, pointed at the drains and nodded sagely as they inspected a telegraph pole. Then some more grey-haired men in big cars followed by one in a cheaper car with a clipboard. I pictured the host of meetings offstage where every little detail was teased out and as much chargeable time was wasted as possible.

Then one morning a van with two workers in overalls turned up and the work began in earnest, though not before lunch of course. And during the lunch break some rain fell, which made starting work impossible, so the next hour was spent loading the spades, wheelbarrow and drills back into the van. Progress was agonisingly or hilariously slow, depending on whether you are a French tax payer or not. Every morning I watched the van turn up and the men sit in it for twenty minutes before getting out and taking a break. Then it was time to open the back of the van and look in it, I think to identify what piece of equipment they needed but didn't have. A few phone calls followed and then a coffee in Le Bar des Arcades while they waited for another van to come from a town fifty kilometres away.

Susie's car park, meanwhile, with the new planting taking root, started getting busy with tourists, and Susie was anxious that some driver would reverse over the plants. She looked out the window whenever a car drew up, saying 'I have just got to stop worrying, I know.'

'Would a beverage be soothing, Madam?' I said, channelling Jeeves. 'Tea? Coffee?' I had decided it was more fun to be a butler than a carer. Providing a punctilious service was more dignified for all of us than dragging my heels and being resentful that they needed so much help.

When I was preparing the coffee I saw that three boxes of tramadol had appeared in the cupboard by the mugs. The stockpiling had begun. I had been to the pharmacy to pick up Stanley and Susie's prescriptions, and staggered out with a bag that wouldn't look out of place on a sack trolley. The French as a nation consume more pharmaceutical drugs than any other in the world. That could change when Susie died.

By placing the little boxes of drugs in the colour-coded and brail-printed packets alongside the tea cups I wondered whether Susie was sending me a covert message. From now on the mission must be top secret, to protect me. The method was in place, the dosage I have no doubt had been printed out off the Internet, copied and filed in at least two places. At this point it was just about the timing.

NINETEEN

Swansongs

I N ACCORDANCE WITH MY earlier plan, I had made up my mind to make the time go as happily as possible. In addition to my adopted role of butler, I also became sommelier, skivvy and chauffeur to the household. And I went about my duties with enthusiasm. I arrived in the house every morning, and after clearing up the kitchen and putting the washing out to dry, I nipped out to buy the wine and food for dinner.

Susie preferred to cook, though sometimes she just issued instructions from the sofa. I would announce dinner, and with elaborate courteousness hold the back of Stanley's chair and smoothly slide it in as he undertook the complex, time-consuming and painful manoeuvre of sitting down. Then I laid the napkins across their laps, bowed and shimmied off for the wine.

'Red or white, sir?' I shouted.

'I think we'll have white. Is that all right darling?'

Susie nodded. I went to the fridge, removed the bottle and cradled it in two hands to present the label to Stanley.

'Very nice,' he said. I knew that, as I had paid for it.

'Bien choisi,' I said, laying the accent on with a trowel. 'May I compliment you on your choice? Parfait avec le tart du cottage.'

'Marvellous, very good. Carry on,' said Stan – I couldn't tell if he was playing or had enjoyably slipped out of reality, as he loved to do with his model making.

I threw in another bow for fun. I then drew the cork, sniffed it, and returned to pour the wine with an extravagant twist of the wrist.

With them seated and yelling at each other, I darted about the room, and brought the cottage pie to the table. I served from their right-hand side and later removed the empty plates from the same side with an ostentatious flourish.

When I sat down to eat, Stanley asked 'Is there any salt?'

'My sincerest apologies,' I said, and leapt up and reached for the condiment, also picking up pepper, mustard and HP sauce (which I knew he had a soft spot for) as if it were the most pleasurable thing to be asked to do.

After dinner they sat on the sofa and watched the English weather forecast with just a corner of France at the bottom of the screen, and not the corner they lived anywhere near, and stared at the English news, open mouthed at the distant political storms of Brexit and the election, while I silently placed the dirty dishes in the machine and wiped the surfaces.

My services as a butler allowed Susie to throw some drinks parties, which I, drunk on my own idiocy, enthusiastically encouraged.

'Would you do the honours?' Stanley would say to me when the doorbell buzzed with the first guests and he dragged himself away from a six-hour stint on the Sopwith Camel.

'By all means, mon plaisir,' I said and clicked my heels. I had plenty of time before any of them made it up the stairs. I was thinking I should get an apron, although I would have preferred a full uniform, preferably one with tails I could pirouette in before proffering a flute of champagne on a silver salver to Stanley. I furiously polished the glasses, lining them up meticulously on the tray, and went about unpackaging the canapés.

'Hello,' Susie and Stanley croaked at full volume, while I stood behind, waiting to lead the deaf and disabled guests to their seats and wheel the trolley of canapés into range, which was quite short considering they were all either blind, arthritic or both.

There was nothing like the cocktail conversation of octogenarian expats. Think of pulling a dead horse across a ploughed field in heavy sleet. It wasn't quite that much fun. One thing I did learn was that however old, no one actually died of boredom. I nodded and smiled and clapped my hands as if I were savouring the repartee of Noël Coward. Every bungled attempt at a funny story, and every punchline suddenly forgotten at the crucial moment, was met with a shriek of pure delight from me. And I lost count of the number of times Stanley said 'Of course the bloody frogs ran away, as they always did,' and I shouted 'Very witty! Well said! By god that's funny.'

I wasn't being sarcastic. I was just determined to be relentlessly upbeat. In their bent forms – and lame, repetitive conversation – I could see my future coming towards me. This was how I was going to be in a couple of decades. Maybe sooner. I wanted to cut them some slack, and at the same time squeeze every last drop of fun, however silly, from the time we all had together. Also, living with people who took ten minutes to get a glass from the fridge and spilt wine on the counter trying to fill it made me think I was in better condition than I thought. I could do that in about ten seconds. I was 60 and careworn, but in that house, I felt young and carefree.

Susie soon discovered that being infirm and old made her invitations difficult to refuse more than twice. She kept going until everyone she knew – and many she didn't – had come to see her. Sometimes the wrinkly invitees turned up to drinks with their own children, who were glum and obedient, themselves nearing retirement age, and had been forced to waste a week of valuable annual leave to travel to one of the most uneventful places on earth to check up on the parentals and deal with the hassles of decaying houses and bodies. Needless to say, for most expats, the gloss had gone off living in La Belle France with the slump in the pound, looming Brexit and laws around inheritance tax that tied in knots those English who wanted to favour one child over the rest. Every expat who came for drinks turned out to be trying to sell their house. Only Susie and Stanley were committed to staying – in their own way.

The happiest party was the day some good news had been received from Britain: property prices were on the slide. Yes, UK property was officially going down, and this gladdened the hearts of every English expat around the globe who had sold up in Blighty, bought abroad and then watched with stoney sunburnt faces the value of the house they had sold in the UK rocket, while their new place stagnated.

My mother took control of the conversation at the drinks parties, where with an audience trapped either by immobility or good manners, and most were disadvantaged by both, she let rip.

There was quite a lot of ground to cover, so interruption was not allowed. The municipal car park planting, and the difficulty and COST of watering it, had to be explained. She made out that the gift of the water from her tap to the village to keep the berberis alive was on a level with Andrew Carnegie's libraries to Scotland. She then moved straight on to her recent book, published six years ago, a memoir, and the favourable reviews of it. Then it was on to the garden at her last house, followed by a quick round-up of anything that had been ill-organised and needed condemnation … bringing her back to the mayor and the planting, which – had she not been on hand – he would have made a mess of. There were one or two impromptu tangents that she couldn't resist, which usually included either famous or rich people she had befriended in the area. There was a popular historian with a holiday home close to where Susie had lived whose name Susie could weave into absolutely *any* story.

One of the salient features of Susie's conversation, or should I say monologues, for that was what her cocktail parties became, was repetition. Alone with me, Susie had the grace, or front, I never knew which, to preface a story she had told me about thirty-two times with the words 'Did I tell you about the time …'

And one of the most well-worn phrases I heard people saying to Susie was 'Yes, I think you did mention that,' along with 'so you said the other day …' meaning ten minutes ago. But neither made the slightest interruption to her flow. One to one she had to occasionally at least pretend to listen briefly to what the other person was saying, but with a small audience she was lethal. Standing at attention with the bottle in my hand and my other arm behind my back scanning for empty glasses I had time to observe her method and work out why she did it.

I personally feared telling a story twice to the same person. I hated noticing that blend of dawning recognition, embarrassment and then pity cross my interlocutors' faces, which in turn made me stutter and fumble for a way to get out of the story as fast as I decently could without making it too different to the last time I told it, or admit what was going on. Since spending time with Susie I found myself looking into my friends' eyes and listening to their laughter, wondering whether they were enjoying my anecdote for the first time or just being kind.

Susie, on the other hand, shamelessly and deliberately repeated herself because she loved it, and she could. Imagine sitting in front of five people listening delightedly with rapt attention to a story that reflected really well on you, as Susie's tended to do, for the third time. She had her own trumpet and she was sodding well going to blow it, and if you got the kind of reaction she received, so would you. None of them could leave. Half of them couldn't even stand up.

Absolutely nobody complained. Me included. Quite the reverse. We pretended we were hearing the anecdotes for the first time. How we all chuckled with delight at the telling of the hilarious time the biographer pulled out his fridge plug to put his electric toothbrush on charge because he had to have a special toothbrush he was on TV so much, and he forgot to put the fridge plug back in and in the morning his milk had gone off.

She was magnificent and indomitable. Each detail was greeted with an impressed ooh, a sigh of open jealousy, or a tinkle of friendly laughter. Maybe the guests' memories were so bad they had forgotten the stories, but I very much doubt it. Susie's stories had a habit of sticking in the mind. Particularly after ten tellings.

She blew her own trumpet, loudly and often, even though her repertoire was small, revelling in the fact that she was protected from interruption simply by being old. She knew perfectly well that her friends were too polite even to hint they had heard her tell four times over the one about the hilarious time she had taught the biographer to cook veal blanquette and he had burnt the onions, before she doubled back for good measure to the village car park with its trees that had now become so diseased in the retelling that they had to be felled not to improve Susie's view but for reasons of health and safety. Only two tellings later Susie had averted the near certain disaster of the trees crashing onto the packed school bus.

The tunes she played on her trumpet were the songs from the album of her own life. Her greatest hits. She told her entranced audiences about the time she met Jeffrey and Mary Archer, the lunch when Shirley Williams turned up, and she blew older tunes from her and my father's undergraduate days at Oxford, about Anthony Crossland, Christopher Chataway and Freddy Raphael, names that meant little or nothing to the hotchpotch of expats at her drinks parties who in the UK had been plumbers, or in the army, or fitted satellite dishes. Then she changed the mood with protest songs from the peace group, and out came the chestnut about the day Bruce Kent and Diane Abbot came to one of her meetings, and a letter of thanks from the Bishop of Gloucester was passed with extraordinary reverence and patience around the cocktail party.

She was scared that no one would blow her trumpet after she was dead. That it would lie silent, tarnished and dented. She was singing her swansong. She was telling anyone who would listen: I have lived on this earth for eight decades, and I lived a life of events and consequences. I had a great garden. I travelled the world. And I knew these celebrities and they knew me. My trumpet may fall silent when I die. But hear it now.

TWENTY

Pushing the boat out

A LONE WITH HER IT was sometimes possible to break out of the orbit of one of her subjects, but it never lasted long.

'Look at how beautifully the light falls on the landscape at this time of the evening,' I tried, staring out of the window at a sunset replete with god rays. The flanks and curves of the hills, unnoticeable in the bright light of the day, emerged as the sun started to dip, and the shadows lengthened, bringing hills, combes, woods, individual trees, valleys, slopes, barns and steeples out of their hiding places.

'Yes. The clouds are wonderful from this room,' she said. 'Now those bloody trees are gone. I'm glad you finally agree with me.'

'It's a perfect orientation for a long view,' said I, ignoring the provocation. 'South-southwest. You always see the sunset but are not blinded by the glare.'

'Did I tell you,' she said 'Gilbert has had to put new blinds up in his sitting room because he finds the afternoon light so strong?'

I couldn't say *Yes. Three times, actually. They are beige. He had a fight with the fitter because he didn't use the one you recommended.* Agonising as it was, I wanted Susie to have the fun of running the little disaster that she had predicted past me for the fourth, and who knew, possibly last time.

'I did tell him not to use Trina's son, but he had his own ideas,' she said. 'He made a complete mess of them. After Gilbert told me what had happened and how much he was charged I called Trina and told her what a drunken ass her son was.' Susie looked out of the window. I suspect she enjoyed that call. Then she added 'In the evening Trina rang up and apologised.' She peered down at the car park. 'I think one of the berberis has been stolen.'

'I doubt that, Mummy. They are quite small. They're not the sort of things thieves nick. Thieves are more interested in things like car radios and strimmers.'

'If one word sums up my life, it should be justice,' she said to me, turning from the window and crabbing towards the fridge. 'And if I had the power, there are two major things that I know I should put right now.'

You might be thinking Global Warming and Racism, but Susie's causes were more important: publicly exposing the garden centre that had sent her the wrong height of berberis and (and this was what made it a matter of principle) had refused to apologise. The other major injustice she had to correct was not getting paid by the mayor for the water that she was supplying from her basement pipe for the Commune's car park planting scheme. She had met a bit of a brick wall with the town hall on this one, so she was going to get the pipe fitted with a *comptoir* so she could work out its cost, publicise it, and in Ghandi-like defiance, NOT ask for a refund.

But after explaining that to me she said 'I think I am going to have to let them go. These wrongs. I have fought all my life for right, but now I must just let them go and surrender.'

I observed her out of the corner of my eye. Was I really the witness to this hugely significant turning point? *Let go? Surrender?* These were phrases I had only heard on her lips when she was ridiculing someone for doing either. Her surrender flag was white on one side, and on the other said FOOLED YOU!

But here she was; possessed of self-knowledge and an understanding of the time ahead of her, she had pushed the wooden boat away from the bank, let slip the painter and was being taken by the gentle current down river into dusk and then night. No shouting, no bailing out, no paddling. Softly spinning as she slid under branches draped with creepers.

I smiled calmly, then grimaced. I thought, there is absolutely zero chance of that happening. She was saying that entirely for effect. She would not waft downstream on the gentle current, she would furiously secure the rope to a tree, scrabble ashore up the greasy bank, hack down an acre of virgin forest and plant it up with berberis.

I had read that cannabis reversed the ageing process, so it seemed a good time to go out onto the terrace to roll and smoke a fat spliff to test the theory and see if it made Susie and Stanley any younger.

TWENTY ONE

In orbit

W E WOULD OCCASIONALLY GO on a day trip, which allowed me to play chauffeur. I much preferred acting like an exclusive limousine driver than being a reluctant grown up son roped into caring for his aged parents.

A popular destination was the hearing-aid shop. The other place Susie liked to motor was to her car park, to inspect the planting. I brought the car to the front door, leapt out of the driver's seat and rushed round the back to open the passenger door and stand to attention as she took two minutes to sit down, and then five minutes to get her legs in, before closing it with exaggerated care and a neat bow and hurrying round the back to get in the driver's seat.

I then very gently drove down to the car park. It was sixty yards away but we didn't have the two hours it would take to do it on foot. I asked for precise instructions as to where to park and which way to point, and my mother directed me with her bony digit. I went forward and reversed about three times to position us. It was quite fun. Then I jumped out and hurried round the back of the car to open her door and offer my arm formally for her to lift herself up on.

I thought the inspection of the plants would mean a brief look while I stood around wishing I had worn a black suit and had a cloth to polish the car. But no, it meant a walk down the entire 100 metres of the new scheme, counting every plant. She did it three times. It took ages because we had a double problem: moving with difficulty and easily losing count.

We ended up staring at an empty patch of ground between two rocks. We were a berberis short and this surely was where it had been removed from. I watched her struggle with her emotions. She didn't know whether to mourn her loss or gloat over me being wrong. I had this idea that Susie was going to ask me to drive her to the Gendarmerie to report its theft. She would stand hunched, but determined, at the counter demanding officers be taken off the totally unnecessary Islamic terrorist surveillance unit and put in shifts on the Castelnau berberis case.

When we returned home we enjoyed a conversation on a lighter subject than berberis that we often fell into chatting about: suicide.

'Did I tell you I had thought of drowning?' she said. 'Throwing myself off a boat, well both of us did,' she quickly added. 'Not that we look like going on any cruise now …'

I pictured the two of them after a long dinner at the Captain's table, shuffling across the deserted deck to the rail, and staring down into the churning waters of the ship's wake. To starboard, the sheer Norwegian cliffs plunged thousands of feet into the black water.

Susie gave the signal. Hold on. I've spotted a flaw. Just how the hell were those two going to get up and over that rail? Stanley could barely make the three inch step back into the house from the terrace, and Susie was hard pressed to get a cup out of a high kitchen cupboard. One might help shove the other up and over, but then be left behind on deck. Maybe they would grimly agree that only one would go. Stanley suggested tossing a coin. Susie shook her head. 'That won't be necessary, *I* will make the sacrifice. *You* go.'

Back in the kitchen she was putting leftovers into a plastic bag, which she held up.

'I always thought one of these with gas in it was going to be too fiddly … too methodical, calculating … You know it's what Barnaby did?' She put a clip on the top and pushed off from the sink to begin the arduous trip to the fridge.

'Yes, I guessed that.' I sighed and tried to brighten up the conversation. 'It's a pity about Switzerland,' I said.

'There is a local euthanasia group around here,' Susie said, opening the fridge and positioning the half-potato. 'But you pay them lots of money and they are not even there at the end.' They sounded interesting, I thought.

Enterprising. Monetising the assisted-suicide game. I took my hat off to them.

'It's a great shame the doctor no longer prescribes barbiturates,' she said. 'It would have made it so much easier. Shall we see what's on the telly?'

A trip to the supermarket with the two of them was like mounting an attempt on Eiger by the north face. Stanley had never in his life taken any exercise for the sake of it and claimed it to be the secret of his longevity. 'I never had any muscles to waste away,' he explained with a sweet smile. His life had been spent in the office and working with his hands. But it did mean the man moved slowly. And when I say slowly I mean at the speed of a slug on tramadol. Stanley also suffered from vertigo whenever he left the house, so standing on the threshold of the front door he looked at the five feet of gravel to the car as though it were a frayed rope bridge over a yawning crevasse.

At Leclerc, Stanley had to remind me to take the carrier bags. It was a bit depressing having my memory jogged by a man of 89. I wondered whether dementia was catching. In the supermarket it was decided by the expedition leader, Susie, that Stanley was too frail for the final push into fruit and vegetables, and he was sent back to the car with me, while she went solo for the summit via toiletries. Stanley and I abandoned a plan to buy him a pair of trousers. I had wanted to do it so I could say *Get a smaller pair so you'll grow into them.*

After the rigours of a thirty-yard hike back to the car with only five stops to rest, Stanley steadied himself on the wing mirror to catch his breath. He looked old and doddery, hunched forward, as though interested in what I was saying about it being cooler in the car, but getting nothing. He blinked. There was a lot of turkey neck. I helped him into the car thinking I was going to have to rewrite the odds. He definitely looked more likely to go first. A surprise winner. The favourite pipped at the post. The bookies delirious. I also had to lengthen Susie's odds, as, though quickly exhausted, she still had a spark of life in her eyes.

Stanley and I waited in the car for Susie's appearance at the sliding doors, like mountaineers staring up at a mountain for their overdue colleagues.

I liked being alone with Stanley. He sat very still and watched the people crossing to and from the shopping cart shed without feeling the need to comment. Some went back to their cars because they forgot the token that unchained the cart. I let out a long fart on three ascending notes. Breaking wind was one of the enjoyable features of being in Stanley's company. Since the last fall he had mysteriously lost his sense of smell and he was too hard of hearing to pick up a plangent anal diphthong discharged right in front of him. On our own, at home, in the middle of the conversation I would let rip a buttock flapper and he would mumble on oblivious.

When a woman went by with a cart loaded with a young family's groceries, he said in a fluting, almost pious tone, 'I have the sculptor's interest in the human form unadorned by clothes. I make it my work to imagine what lies under the so-restrictive and unnecessary vestments.'

'I know what you mean,' I said.

Thus the two of us diverted ourselves with a twenty-minute gentleman's perving session. Swathed in the cool of the air conditioning, listening to Stanley's even breathing and occasional grunts of approval, I did not ask myself what on earth I was doing with my life.

I had left Stanley and Susie unattended in Castelnau on only two occasions, and both times something had gone wrong. I didn't know if that was coincidence, but I feared it wasn't. When I was in the vicinity I gave them that little bit of confidence they needed to cope on their own. The first time I was absent Stanley had tripped coming out of the lift and the lift door had banged again and again on his head, trying to close. The other time he had had a funny turn. It made me think about what was going to happen when I did finally leave them. I had a home in Somerset and a life, somewhere. That's why I didn't think about it.

'I sorry. I'm sorry,' Susie said, opening the boot. 'The blasted man made a muddle of my coupons,' she said. 'Idiot.'

'I don't mind,' said Stanley. 'In fact there's something rather inspiring about this place. I might come with you next time and just sit in the car. I think it's done me some good.'

That night I went out onto the terrace to do more research into the effects of smoking dope and ageing. The village had fallen absolutely silent. I had noticed the extraordinary ability of Castelnau to go stone dead at a moment's notice. A few hours earlier there had been tourist camper vans and hire cars jostling with the yellow post vans for parking spaces, French, English and German conversation echoing in the alleys, fast and slow footfalls on the cobbles, and the howl of the village mopeds. Then: nothing. Not even the cooing of pigeons.

I looked up and watched what I first thought was a plane and then identified as a satellite passing silently between the stars across the deep, dark sky. It was a mirror hundreds of miles away sending back a speck of light. Susie, Stanley and I were satellites circling in the black. I was hurtling through the void alongside them, occasionally docking, but otherwise locked in the same silent orbit. I continued to send down signals to the distant planet that was Existence-Before-Geriatric-Parents, hoping they were picked up. But along with the millions of other carers, whose old lives went on without them being there to enjoy them, far far away, there seemed little chance of rescue. I watched the world upside down through a triangular window, and wondered what was going on under that quilted cloud. Getting back down there rested on a rescue mission with an untested low-budget propulsion system called Ryanair, delivering one of my siblings, contact with whom had grown increasingly unreliable during my months in France.

Stanley and Susie's satellites occasionally sent off intelligible messages. I heard Stanley say to Susie 'She's not young! She's 80!' But otherwise their flickering logic boards were beginning to fail, and both were going to decay into space junk, slowly drop out of orbit, fall suddenly to earth and burn out.

I sent the end of the spliff spinning towards the car park, stood up, and went in to clear up dinner.

TWENTY TWO

Snow in May

A FEW DAYS LATER STANLEY collapsed. I received a message on my phone from Susie and hurried through the cloisters to their house. I imagined him surrounded by anxious pompiers while they worked on his heart. I would shout 'Let me through! I'm a writer!' and wave my notebook.

I found the two of them on the top landing, Susie helping Stanley from the lift to the bedroom.

'What's happened?' I asked.

'I wasn't too good this morning,' he said in barely intelligible words. 'I can only walk with one leg.' I went ahead of his walker getting the furniture out of the way, and then helped him onto the bed.

As I tucked him in, he said 'I never thought of you as a carer.'

I went to get him a glass of water, though drinking water, like taking exercise, was an activity the Stanley considered injurious to his health.

'Drink this, please,' I said. 'Please.' I drew the covers carefully over him.

Susie entered the room impatiently. I had the sense that she thought I might be making it worse by taking it too seriously.

'I think he's had a stroke,' I said.

'I think I have,' he mumbled.

'I don't believe he's had a stroke,' she said to me. And to Stanley, 'Who's the prime minister?'

He had a think, and then said 'Snow.'

'You see?' she said. 'He hasn't had a stroke.'

'I told you I wouldn't make it to 90,' Stanley croaked.

'You've only got four days,' Susie said. 'Make an effort. I'm going to close the door. I'll be downstairs.'

She went downstairs to do the thing she found most useful in a crisis: make lists. In this case for his 90th birthday party. Guests, food, drink, placement.

I went downstairs and said 'Er, the Prime Minister is Teresa May, not someone called Snow. There isn't even a Snow in the cabinet.'

She did not appear to hear me.

I gave up smoking dope. It didn't make me – or them – feel younger. I went on to the hard stuff: tramadol. It's basically the only way I could work with the elderly. While Susie started putting together a 90th birthday party, with the joyful creation of a list of guests who were to be excluded from it, I sneaked to the mug cupboard and snaffled a couple of pills. It sweetly rounded the sharp edges of every irritation. But at what a cost.

Every trammy I took extended my mum's life, and my stay in France, by a few days.

I went upstairs, knocked on Stanley's door and entered the light-filled room, where he lay as I had left him, but reading a book.

'Hello,' he said.

'You're not dead?' I asked.

'No, no, far from it.'

'Do you need anything?'

'I'm quite used to this,' he smiled. 'I spent a lot of time alone in bed as a child. I was sickly.'

I sat down to listen.

'My father was a bully. He only ever taught me two things: to develop photographs and to serve at a cocktail party. I was made to do as I was told, and be seen and not heard.'

It was a few verses of his swan song. Of his pulling together the strands of his life in an attempt to tie them neatly; or, at least, not to leave them *too* tangled. His song was quite different to Susie's. It was not blown loudly on a trumpet but played quietly, and I sensed a little mournfully and regretfully, on a muted French horn.

He was born into a naval family when the British navy was still a meaningful phrase. His home was a manly environment intensified by the fact that there had been no female children in three generations. Stanley himself had just one female descendant, a granddaughter in the United States who he saw rarely but doted on. There were several photos of her around the house, which Susie moved because she thought they cluttered up the place. It was unfortunate that Stanley found himself in such a patriarchy, because he was a sensitive, rather feminine man, whose talents lay more in the direction of making art rather than war. His family didn't know what to do with him, and after reading law at Cambridge he was shunted into accountancy. He was in the last generation who didn't make their passion their profession, so he kept sculpture, drawing and photography hidden as pastimes while pursuing a *sensible* career. He had ended up an accountant to people in show biz and had many famous clients, none of whom he mentioned in conversation.

The first sculpture he created, at night school, of a naked woman looking slightly anxious stood on the kitchen island. ('I love my delicate touch on the pubes,' Stanley once remarked to me.)

We talked for half an hour about his childhood, then he picked up the *Radio Times*, studied the remote control, stabbed at its buttons, stared at the screen, tipped his head back onto the pillow and went to sleep. On the bedside table rested a pair of binoculars which I found him using during Wimbledon for the women's doubles.

'I am just checking the score,' he had said, lifting his G&T with two fingers in the glass.

I watched him doze before going about my duties. He was getting frailer, and less mobile, almost hourly.

I guessed one day he'd just go from his bed to his wheel-chair and never walk again. There was talk that the doctor thought he might have dementia or even Alzheimer's, but all I noticed was a gentle slowing and softening. He was a suit that had got baggy at the knees and elbows with wear. But he was still serviceable as Stanley.

Snow. May. I could see the tenuous connection and kind of understood his mistake. Something to do with the weather and the seasons. The decaying mind was viewed as a calamity, like a pancaked apartment block with people trapped between the floors, but I saw Stanley's as a picturesque ruin, and a ruin is sometimes more beautiful than the original building.

I would have loved to have taken a tour around Stanley's crumbling thoughts and clambered over his rotten memory, which I pictured as a roofless mansion. Gazing up at the stone wall I would spot the holes that had once held the joists that had supported the events of the previous ten days. But they, along with most of last month, had disappeared. Higher up I would notice the exposed fireplace of his childhood bedroom, with the sunshine hitting a triangle of wallpaper in the exact spot it did 82 years ago. Ambling across the carpet of grass I would come across an opening with gouges in the stone where the hinges had been torn out that had once held the heavy door of Stanley's first wedding day. I doubted he had a photo of that, or even whether one existed any more. His first wife was dead, and probably most of the guests had either died or forgotten that wedding day. I decided to get Stanley to describe it to me so that I could retain a mental image when all others had faded.

Stanley was spending more time ambling around the ruin which to him had become a bit of a labyrinth. Like collapsed dry-stone walls, words and meanings were slipping and old memories spilling out. One of them was his 'accident-prone' Uncle Bill.

'He was an admiral who lost two destroyers on the Malay peninsula between the wars. The first one he ran aground on sand banks in an estuary and the second he rammed into the waterfront at night. Lovely man,' Stanley piped. 'Complete idiot.'

Stanley's hearing wasn't so good, but had not deteriorated as much as I had thought. Later that evening I came up from the laundry room and heard him say to Susie: 'Why has no one ever taught Guy how rude it is to fart all the time?'

TWENTY THREE

Bunbury

ALGERNON, IN OSCAR WILDE'S *The Importance of Being Ernest*, had a fictitious invalid friend in the country called Bunbury, who he used to pretend to visit to escape social engagements. A Bunbury was an essential tool for any Englishman living amongst the expat community in France, with its lively appetite for deadly dinner parties. Susie and Stanley became my Bunbury, and I used them as an excuse not to go somewhere in direct proportion to the number of invitations I received. I had one particularly persistent friend to whom I gave a totally unrealistic idea of how much work they were to look after. Claudia was a stout, spoilt Italian who I had met at a party in London and who planned to come and find me in Somerset until I informed her that I was in France looking after my ailing mother. I had no desire to spend any time in her abrasive company, so I told her that I would be in touch when, well, when things either stabilised or ... I left the idea of imminent death hanging in the air.

But Claudia was soon in touch again. Could I get the time off for a weekend in Rome? She had checked the flights from Toulouse and there were two or three a day, so even an overnight visit was practical.

'Unfortunately my stepfather's not been too well. I just don't think it's a good time to leave them,' I told her in a phone call from my friend Dave's house in the Ariège, where I had been staying for a few days. Stanley and Susie seemed to be getting on fine without me.

'*Mai!* Why don't you make for one night? Why don't you provide them a nurse? You are so mean Guy. You are tight. Cheap. My assistant can find you one. Then you can leave your mamma and stepfather in safe hands.'

'Impossible,' said I. 'It could happen at any moment. I'm sure you understand. I want to be here for it when it does.' I had lowered my voice as though I were at that moment in the death chamber. I think I even said 'It could be time for the priest quite soon.'

If you knew Claudia, you would perhaps have a bit more sympathy. She was a rich Italian woman who liked to get her own way and seemed to enjoy bullying for the sake of it. For some unaccountable reason her avaricious eye had fallen on me. I could never explain it. I said I was very sorry I couldn't get away, whispering urgently, 'I've got to go now', as though the doctor had summoned me upstairs. I switched off the phone and continued chatting to Dave.

Two weeks later Claudia rang and I absentmindedly accepted the call before checking who it was from.

'How is your mamma?' she asked.

'She's doing as well as can be expected,' I said, watching Susie shouting from her balcony at some council workers who were fixing the hosepipe for the berberis in the wrong place.

'Bene. You are come to Roma for a weekend? My friend Gianni is 'aving a party at the best sushi in the city. You fall in love to Gianni, 'e ees so funny. He goes into every restaurant and drop his pant; everybody laughs ee so funny. We were laughing so loud. Everybody loves Gianni.' I thought I might possibly be an exception to that rule.

'I would love to. He sounds ... such fun. But I'm afraid I cannot possibly leave my mother at this time.'

'All right. No problem. You cannot travel. I will come to you. I get my assistant to book me a flight and I will make a taxi. You can take me a hotel in your village.'

'Well, er ..,' I had to be careful what I said now. 'OK. They have improved a little actually. But I'm going to be busy cooking and looking after them. They are practically incapable and almost totally ga-ga.'

She dragged a date out of me.

I sat down Stanley and Susie and grimly briefed them.

'The only way this is going to work,' I said, 'is if you two pretend to be *much* older and more infirm than you are, OK? Or Claudia will smell a rat, and frankly I am scared of her.'

I felt I left them fully aware of the gravity of the situation, and believed I could count on them.

I picked Claudia up at Toulouse–Blagnac Airport. 'You know you look stupid like that,' were her first words. 'This pants make your belly look so big and hugly. You know? And those shoes. The look like a pig. Why do you English wear always ugly shoes? Always. For shoes you have to go to Puglio. To Carlo. He is my friend. 'Is family 'ave been making shoes for my family for two 'ondred years.'

'How wonderful for them,' I said.

I thought what I would do was sweep Claudia around to Susie and Stanley's for a *brief* hello at the beginning of her trip (which had been extended to two nights); establish the two invalids, and basically Bunbury the hell out of them for the next three days.

I let Claudia and myself into Susie's house.

I lowered my voice, 'We won't stay long. They both tire very quickly and the doctor has advised me not to let them get stressed.'

We advanced into the hall to the bottom of the stairs. I called up to the first floor, where the kitchen, sitting room and terrace are. 'Hello. How are the patients today?'

Then I heard the most ghastly combination of noises I could ever have imagined: the pop of a champagne cork and the croak of old people laughing. Claudia raised her eyebrows.

'Sounds like they're having one of their rare good days,' I said, and trudged up the stairs.

Stanley and Susie stood in the centre of the living room in freshly ironed clothes, their hair immaculate.

While I miserably made the introductions I watched Stanley charge four glasses of champagne, and then pick up and offer around triangles of toast with foie gras. My mother had a twinkle in her eye.

We were ushered out onto the terrace, where Claudia admired my mother's plants, exclaiming 'You never said what a wonderful gardener your mother is.'

'I used to have a real garden,' Susie said, 'in my last house …' and she was off. I went through to get biscuits and more drink from time to time and each time I returned Claudia said something like 'You never told me your mother was a film producer …' or 'you should have said your mother ran a successful restaurant.' Or '… was a leading figure of the political left.'

Meantime Stanley, who looked dashing in a pale blue shirt and white trousers, behaved himself so ridiculously well, I was stunned into a state of numbness.

'It is such a pleasure to entertain a woman of such discernment and culture,' he said, topping up her glass.

And when Susie said to Stanley, 'What would you like with your drink?' he replied 'Just a touch of your sweet lips.' He wasn't even too hammy. 'I used to climb over in bed and grab her,' he said to Claudia of Susie. 'Now I just reach out to check she's not dead.'

To make matters a lot worse Susie said 'Maybe you two would like to stay for supper. Nothing complicated. I'm sure what we have will have will stretch easily.'

'No!' I wanted to shout. But Claudia was under Susie's spell. 'If it is no trouble, why not? Is actually so charming out here on this terrace, and your parents are so sympatico Guy. But only if you are not too tired.'

'No!' they said in unison. 'It's lovely to have some company apart from Guy. He is so boring.'

My mother then served roasted quail in bacon, with a fennel and onion side dish. She obviously had them already cooked.

'But this is meravigliosa,' Claudia said. 'You never said your mamma was such a good cook. Susie, this quail is perfecto. Under normal circumstances, for quail you have to go to Livorno. To my friend Peitro's restaurant. His family have shot and killed quail for my family for hundreds of years. His are beyond compare. But outside Livorno, this is the finest quail I have ever tasted. Brava Susie!'

I managed to get Claudia out of the house, and then of course it really started: 'But why did you say you mother was a little old lady who was so ill? She is fantastic. So strong and so capable. And 87! You are so lucky. She is so full of life and ideas and so charming. And Stanley. He is not as you said he was at all. For a start he is so handsome. And such a gentleman ...'

As we walked back towards the hotel I noticed the swollen champagne corks dotting the pavement under Susie's terrace which Stanley had sent flying over the trellis.

'And your mother has had such a hardeness in her life! She had to manage four children on solo and only 38 when your papa die. And yet she has achieve so much! And is such an incredible woman! Questa inspiratzione! Guy you are ungrateful. You know really I think you are a 'orrible man. Such a shame. Veramente. A bad son. Now where is my hotel? You know is very 'orrible as well. You book me for the worst room in the whole place. And actually it is a dump as a matter of fact.'

TWENTY FOUR

Total war

FOR HER 87TH BIRTHDAY I bought Susie a watch, as the tiny six-sided one I had known since I was a boy had become unreadable with her eyesight. I wrote on her birthday card *Lots of love and Lots of Time,* thinking that even if it was short it could still be abundant.

Celebrations were muted because Stanley's 90th had been so exhausting. As Stanley and I said *Many happy returns,* I wondered how silly that was. Wasn't this scheduled to be her last birthday?

But *was* she going to Opt Out? Obviously it was her plan, and she had always been a woman for whom a plan was a military tank which she drove through the shanty town of life, scattering those it didn't squash under it.

When I had last spoken to her, sitting outside on the terrace, she had mentioned an obstacle. 'It's Stanley. I can't leave Stanley behind ...' It was true that when I arrived Stanley had been looking after her, and that the table had now turned. Or the bed tray to be more accurate. It looked like remaining that way.

She flinched. 'What's that noise?' she asked.

Someone close by had started playing Prokofiev at high volume.

We have not spoken about the birds. Susie left Britain, flounced out I think is the appropriate term, in 1990. She had silenced the howling outboard engines of the powerboat club, but surprisingly had failed to close the United States Air Force Base, and could no longer live with the noise or the shame.

She and Stanley had bought a farmhouse in the Tarn, an hour from Toulouse, on top of a hill surrounded by hundreds of square kilometres of forest and farmland. The nearest road was a three-car-a-day single track lane and well out of earshot. There were no lakes or flightpaths to worry about. Nothing could go wrong this time. What few buildings you could see were ruins or bankrupt farmhouses, unlikely to be reoccupied, except possibly by a member of the British middle classes relocating to France, but they too were looking for peace and quiet. The farmhouse at the bottom of the hill was bought by an English woman, whose hobby was the keeping and breeding of tropical birds.

I remember going to see Susie sometime in about 1993 and being led outside first thing in the morning. It was a glorious cloudless day and the blue sky stretched far and wide over the broccoli of the forest. I assumed I had been brought there to admire the splendour of the ineffably peaceful scene.

'Do you hear that?' she asked.

'What?' said I.

'That. That ghastly noise.'

Oh no, I thought. Not again. This is how it had been for years back in Fairford with the powerboats. She had spent my teens stalking around the house with a decibel meter, a brick-sized machine with a dial that she stared at hoping to get a good reading, which she then entered into her log, a diary kept solely to record something that really annoyed her. She used to make us shut up so she could properly hear the disturbance. I strained my ears to hear her nuisance.

'What is it?' I asked.

'A macaw, or cockatoo. The worst is the bird of paradise. An absolutely horrible screeching, nasty sound.'

'It's quite a long way away,' I pointed out.

'It's a clear nuisance. In British law I could take out an injunction. I am seeing a French lawyer later this week.'

'Really?' I said.

'Of course,' she said. 'It has to be stopped.'

Thus was war declared. She used tactics she had honed in her battles against the CIA, the USAF and the powerboat club. Like most conflicts, it was the civilians who suffered most. Susie's family and friends were all conscripted. Conscientious objectors were crushed. Censorship was introduced on the home front. Here were some proscribed phrases:

Is that it?

I can't hear anything.

Wow those birds sound amazing!
But that's quite a nice noise.
Can't you just ignore it?

Susie attempted to mobilise the French version of the RSPB, which she told to take out a prosecution on grounds of animal cruelty, but they weren't interested. I seem to recall Susie toying with the idea of a takeover of the entire organisation to get it to change its ruling. This was total war. She had a black ops campaign which sent any new arrival at her house down to recce the enemy with some cover story or another, so she could locate a weakness in their defences. She even tried to access the zookeeper's tax records – I am not sure how. I am absolutely certain that if Susie could have bugged the house and phone line, she would have, in true CIA style.

It took two years of legal and personal harassment to get the poor woman to quit with her birds and relocate to a house a few kilometres further down the valley. I quake even now to write *poor woman* for fear of reprisals for fraternising with the enemy.

The birds were the last of Susie's litigations if you don't count a few skirmishes relating to my father's literary estate which she took on just for the fun of squeezing off a couple of injunctions. She wasn't called Sue for nothing. Downsizing to the new house in Castelnau with its level floors, modest terrace and practical lift was a sign we all thought that she was now past cooking up a dispute, but we were wrong. She went straight into the tree-felling controversy. That was now over. Neighbourly legal actions were surely a thing of the past, or so I thought until the evening in the middle of the heatwave when we were out on the terrace talking about her having to look after Stanley rather than waving goodbye. Stanley had now joined us and we were consuming our usual three bottles of wine before dinner when from an open window over the narrow street came a sustained burst of Prokofiev's trumpet and timpani.

Susie jumped with shock as she did at every loud noise, whether it was a car skidding on the gravel, or a moped whining through the street below. She was always making a point. I sometimes thought that not ignoring a nuisance was the primary purpose of her existence.

'That's at least 100 decibels,' she said.

The music was so loud that even Stanley heard it, which was saying something. The neighbour obviously had no idea of the waterfall of pain he was about to step under playing music this loud at this distance from my mother. He would be another notch on her decibel meter, another broken man to add to the list begun by the maitre d' at the Ngorongoro Crater Hotel. I saw my mother slipping into battle mode. I would have imagined her reaching into the cupboard for her gun, breaking it and checking the barrels with a beady eye. Now I pictured her at her desk, ringing up the old noise-nuisance team. The private eye who could hack anyone and anything, now retired and lying by his pool in Miami, who is drawn back into the game by Susie. Then we see the Prof., a noise measurement boffin with a shock of grey hair, who takes Susie's call in his lab, and is intrigued by the technical challenge. Then it's the lawyer, the one who was a rookie on the powerboats, and who after the Air Force debacle swore he'd never work for a maverick like Susie again, but was drawn in to the UK–EU implications of the aviary case and won acclaim for the victory. He was now a senior partner at a major international law firm, but dropped a 100 million dollar commercial lawsuit to go to Susie's side, where there was a hint of an appropriate but undeniable and definitely unacted upon sexual frisson which had always existed between the attorney and this client, with her unbridled lust for casual litigation.

An explosion of Stravinsky from the window over the street made the crockery in Susie's kitchen fizz and a smile play upon her face as she went about preparing dinner, relishing the prospect of a swift victory in an open-and-shut case. Unfortunately, the neighbours on the other side of the maniac called the police, and the music stopped mid-track, never to be heard again, much to my mother's disappointment. So the final campaign was never fought.

Susie now turned her attention to making lists for the family holiday week coming up in August. We hadn't talked much about death for a few days, until a chance remark I made reintroduced the subject.

'I generally approve of global warming,' I said, 'living in England. But this heat wave is too hot to handle. It makes a mockery of the line *Shall I compare thee to a summer's day?* Unless you disliked the woman.'

'Well, I won't have to worry about it next year,' Susie said.

I took this to mean that the family holiday week was going to be a secret one-sided *a dieu* to all of us lot, and she would be Pushing On Through before next summer.

The weather was still stifling when the grandchildren, now mainly in their 20s, brought round their toddler kids from where they all stayed in a house near Castelnau to visit Susie and Stanley on an informal rota.

I was present when my daughter and son introduced their children to Susie for the first time. As my grandson, Ezra, waddled towards her with his arms outstretched, and my granddaughter, Lola, shyly hid her face in her mum's hair, I saw Susie's face light up with joy. I thought hang on, this is going to change a few things. Living so far from us all, deep in France, where there were so few visits from the family, there was a feeling at Susie's house that it was the end of the genealogical line. Weeks, even months passed when Susie and Stanley didn't see a relative, and it felt as though there was nobody to leave behind, apart from me – and I don't think she worried too much about that. But here in her sitting room was a whole new generation of little Kennaways, who she hadn't annoyed or insulted and who were delighted by her.

It was a great week. Susie seemed so free of her old anxieties, and allowed the squeaking little children to do all the stuff that kids do that had always been so tricky for her to deal with in the past, like not sitting still, forgetting to say thank you, having dirty fingers, pressing buttons, tripping over and spinning on her office chairs. She even processed one evening in Stanley's company out of Castelnau to the country gite and sat in a bendy plastic chair at a long table of Kennaways, and even though there was no formal placement and a long wait between courses while everyone smoked a joint, she found no fault, and seemed to enjoy the chaotic meal on that hot evening under a starry sky scratched rather wonderfully with a meteor shower.

I noticed her carefree happiness, and wondered whether this was the sign that she was letting go of us, and, in a sense, of herself. Was she thinking: *This is my last supper with my children and their children and their children. They will carry the torch forwards now. I hope they remember me as I am on this joyful night.* Knowing she was going to die must have made these encounters particularly poignant.

I had to go back home to Somerset and I packed up my flat after my three-month occupation. The tourists were thinning out and the wind that blew down the cobbled alley was no longer hot. The over-advertised Castelnau summer music festival had come and gone. The second-homers of Britain, Germany and Holland were making good their roof racks, bidding goodbye to their buildings and heading north, their suntans but not their memories of a summer in the Tarn, soon to fade.

And I would miss my apartment. The child on the piano could now play *Ragtime* and *Für Elise* right through without hesitation or mistakes. I would miss her lessons. I would miss the hiss of my neighbour's pressure cooker, and her dog Zorro snuffling into my studio when I left the door open.

With my car loaded, I went over and said goodbye to Susie, and left her waving from her balcony, very much alive and well. In fact, she was looking stronger than when I had arrived all those months ago, and showed little sign that she was about to Draw Down the Curtain, despite the accumulating packs of tramadol. My mission was not accomplished.

Or maybe it was. A fine last summer was an integral part of a good death.

TWENTY FIVE

The belly of the beast

Direction General des Finances Publiques,
Department d'Excesse de Vitesse,
Montauban,
35911
France

Speeding Ticket numero 729/LXC/7653004

Mon Cher Gendarme,

Il est de mon devoir de vous informer que j'écris en tant qu'exécuteur du Last Will et Testament de M. Kennaway. Oui! Monsieur Kennaway est mort! Il keel 'imself dans une accident d'automobile 2 minutes après l'infraction ci-dessus, parce que as you point out he was doing le 32 kmh au-delà de la limite légale, et il sortie de la route et s'esté crasée sur votre road-signe qui dite RALENTIR ou comme on dit en Anglais, SLOW DOWN. Quelle ironique!

J'ai plus de mauvaises nouvelles pour vous: M. Kennaway mort un home sans monnaie. Il etait brassique, ou comme on dit a Londre: le skint. Je n'ai pas le 65 euros nécessaires pour régler cette amende. Je suis tellement telle m'enttellement désolé. Si c'est une consolation, il y a beaucoup d'autres personnes dans votre situation. Un marchand de sauccison local estdû £337,650. Oui, c'est incroiable mais M. Kennaway aime le porc produits beaucoup. Connaissais vous Le Ginster? Je le recommend beaucoup a toute les Gendarmes Français.

M. Kennaway était un auteur de livres. If ee become a best seller après sa mort je weel be able a payer votre inestimable department d'excèsse de vitesse avec les royalties! To help achieve thees s'il vous plait encourager vos gendarmes à acheter des livres de M. Kennaway et leave les reviews de customers positives sur Amazon.

Une dernier faveur, je vous e demande. Would eet be possible a acheter le signe de route que M. Kennaway s'ecrasé into? Nous n'avons pas le monnaie pour une headstone sur la tombe de M. Kennaway et j'ai l'idee a utiliser la signe qui dit RALENTER dans le cimetière. Faites le moi savoir. Je crains que nous can make un offrir de un euro pour eet.

Merci bien pour tout! Especiallament le grand sales drive du livres de M. Kennaway.

Mes plus profound et delicates et fraternal amicalements.

PAUL FRYER BSc (Avocat a gens mort)

I posted that as I left Castelnau. On the road north I remembered that that was not the first time I had killed myself. I had a number of times written – as my executor – to the Metropolitan Police in London to escape paying a parking fine. It had always worked.

Maybe my acceptance of Susie's plan to blow the full-time whistle was connected to my idea that death was not an end but an escape. When my father died I comforted myself with the thought that a month or two later he would burst back through the front door laughing and saying 'Sorry about that kids, I just had to lie low for a bit to get this ruddy producer off my back. The bloody man wouldn't take no for an answer. It was a contractual thing. It was a stupid storyline. I couldn't have done anything decent with it. I'm afraid there was no other way out of it. Come on, give me a hug. Am I pleased to see you!' And I would kiss him and be wrapped in his tobacco and whisky embrace.

But he never came home.

He never came home.

Maybe I should have seen him dead. But we were protected from that sight. A change occurred to me around that time in my life. From then on I felt slightly different from everyone else I met, as though my father had taken a crucial part of me with him. I wondered if it were possible to go over and ask for it back. To get a short snatch of death and ask him a couple of things.

I sailed across the Channel on the Cherbourg to Poole ferry, making a late afternoon crossing on a warm humid day and placid sea. To get a break from the decor – it was no wonder people felt sick on that ship – I went to the rail at the stern and reviewed its height. It reached my chest; way too high for Stanley or Susie, and was fitted with rope netting so I couldn't get a foot onto the metal bars to help myself up and over it, if I wanted to, which I didn't.

I looked down the curved riveted steel of the ferry's belly. Even on such a calm day the veined grey water was terrifying. I thought about tipping myself into it. I wondered if I'd bounce down the side of the ship before I hit the sea. Just that fall would be bad enough. But then the pitiless water. I'd be dragged under quickly, pulled into the vortex of the propeller, despite by this point desperately trying to swim away from the ship to save my life. Death right there. Tugging me towards him. Her. It. Sucked under the surface, I'd hear the grinding of the motor and spinning of the prop, which takes my leg off just below the knee. I'd manage to push my way up to the surface, blood in the water, to see the ferry chugging away. No one saw me go over, or heard my yelp, except for a couple of Brit truckers who didn't mention it because it would only hold them up.

It was a healthy sequence of thoughts. Under normal circumstances I did not want to kill myself. Death was a terrifying, painful thought. Not easeful. When it became thinkable and then doable – that was the time to do it. We all carried a fail-safe device in our heart. We didn't need the state to tell us when we could and when we couldn't kill ourselves. We couldn't, until we had to.

I looked up from the grimy water, and saw the setting sun gilding the Dorset coast, obliging all who looked with some god rays. The land to my right, up ahead, was purple and darkening with dusk. I started making out the twinkling lights of Poole harbour, and imagined cosy pubs on a steep cobbled high street. Through bay windows with swirly glass I could see a fire flickering in the hearth and a young barman reaching for a glass to pour a pint of British ale into. Life. Calling me. That's what it did when things were going OK.

TWENTY SIX

Marvellous pompiers

A WARM, WET WINTER BLEW across Somerset, swamping the glistening fields. I heard little news from France though I saw in a photo that Stanley was now eating from his wheelchair when he always used to transfer to a wicker chair. In a phone call Susie told me that they had managed an outing to IKEA but had turned back after five overwhelming minutes, and had then started looking for their car on the wrong floor of the car park. A painful piece of intelligence to me. I had witnessed the agonising trek including rest stops and deep breathing, from the fridge to the drinks cupboard. And there was a whisky at the end of that one. Lost on the wrong floor of the car park. My mother's back and Stanley's legs both about to go, while they searched for something that wasn't there.

I read the manuscript in front of the fire. This book. The one you are reading now. It wasn't just missing a death. It was missing something else. It was missing what had been going on in my mum's head over the summer. That's what I wanted know. What had she been thinking? Had she really meant it when she said she was going to kill herself? Or was it a game? Were the tramadol tablets going to be popped out of their blister packs all at once on that final morning? And if so, when? I needed to know, and I suspect you do as well. I would have to ask her. And to do that I would have first to inform her that I had been writing this book about her.

That wasn't the most delightful prospect, so I decided to give the plan further reflection. To be honest, my tactic for dealing with my mum over this book was to wait for her to die before showing it to her. Plan B was hoping that her mind would start to disintegrate by the time she got hold of it. Fat chance of that.

The next day but one, I wrote to Susie, telling her that over the summer I had been taking notes and had written them up into a book which I wanted to show her. It was about her plan to kill herself. The project, I said, was very much at an early stage, and could end up novelised, if she thought I had pried too closely into her life. I could make her a man, living in Spain, for instance, to distance her safely from the book. I waited for her answer.

Many thanks for your letter. It is always so good to hear from you, I love your letters, and you sound in a much better place, happier. I was both amused and tickled by your idea of writing of my decease plans.

Actually my hand has been hovering over the Mogadon page on Google very recently, in fact just yesterday. Not in a fit of depression but perhaps in a mood of necessity.

Stanley has been felled by another bout of infection, which is the same as he had 3 years ago that landed him in hospital for so long, but this time he had a fall, because his legs just gave way, and he collapsed in a heap in the doorway of his study. The marvellous pompiers came to pick him up quite late at night, and the doctor came the following day and ordered tests, the results of which were lousy. So, at the moment he is having daily injections of antibiotics and I am hauling him around in a wheelchair. Thank god for the lift. Currently he is swaddled in bed, wearing a cardigan and insisting on an extra (Harrods' best) blanket on the bed because it is cold ... Anyway, I don't mind what you write about me, or how you write about my thoughts of quitting this ridiculous planet.

All my love, happy writing, from Mummy.

I thought: she *may* mind when she reads it. But I decided to print it up and take a trip back to the Tarn to present it to her. I was braced for a few rebuttals. I was braced for a bollocking for my insolence. But I hoped that she would view this book as a small monument to her magnificent, indomitable character and a little addition to the debate about old people and death.

I was shortly to leave for the airport with the manuscript, and decided that rather than recounting what Susie said to me about what I had written, I would allow you, silent reader, to read my mother's own words, without editing or censorship from me. Therefore after she has read the manuscript I will give the next chapter – *in its entirety* – to Susie. She can have two thousand words in which she can, if she wants, put her side of our summer in the Tarn. I am off to see her now, so the next words and the next chapter will be Susie's writing.

TWENTY SEVEN

Plutonium

I T'S STILL ME. I'M up in the spare room. I didn't have the balls to give it to her. The manuscript sits on the bed behind me as I type this, pulsing like a lump of plutonium. On the plane I had a leisurely scan of it that quickly turned feverish. As we came into land I closed my eyes and asked myself why, when Susie ushered me into her bedroom a year ago, did I not just try and persuade her that it was silly talk going on about killing yourself? What idiocy had made me scurry for my notebook?

Doubts and fears twitched like cockroaches by the time I got out of the car into the beating wind, entered Susie's house and walked the gallows to her sitting room. It was late and I had eaten four times on the journey, but Susie had cooked a three-course dinner, so I sat down and tucked into it.

'Did you bring your book? Is that what it is?' she said.

'I'm tired,' I said, swallowing and swallowing again to get a lump of meat down. 'Can I talk to you about it tomorrow?'

Upstairs, I couldn't sleep, and started looking at the document again. I ran through my options. I could throw it out of the window; a whipping wind rattled the shutters and would disperse it far and wide, though there was the danger that in the morning people would find and read the pages and – seeing Susie's name – turn up at the house to return them. The process could go on for days, with Susie placing the pages in order in her study, her mood growing grimmer. I could flush it down the loo, a piece of paper at a time. 89 flushes. I even thought about eating it.

Why hadn't I said some more pleasant things about her? Like the way she and Stanley often sat on the sofa watching TV after dinner, holding hands and talking quietly to each other in a most romantic, loving and charming way, sometimes both of them awake. Why do I always have to add a clause like that at the end of the sentence? And why hadn't I mentioned how often I heard really happy laughter coming from their bedroom. Not saucy laughter, just companionable chuckling. Nor did I mention – why? – the times I went into their room and the two of them were chatting happily while Susie sat in the tub chair with a needle and thread taking in Stanley's trousers as he diminished in size. A loving, kind scene.

I heard the lift go clunk and the door wheeze open. Susie was up, unusually early. I followed her downstairs.

'Have you got it?' she asked.

'Well actually,' I said, 'I had a quick glance at it before I went to bed and I think I need to give it a light polish before showing it to anyone.' I had decided by them to slash about 30 per cent of it.

She said 'Go and get it I want to read it!' Punctuated like that.

I went upstairs, sighed so heavily that it made a raspy whistle, picked the miserable pages off the bed and returned downstairs.

Susie took them, and then sat down at the kitchen table to start reading. For some reason a gif of a boy playing hopscotch in a minefield popped up in my head.

I imagine that some of you readers will be smiling or even laughing at my discomfort, you rotters!

'I am still very much thinking of turning it into a novel,' I said to the top of her head. 'In which case you would be totally unrecognisable. I could call you Steve, and place you on the Costa Blanca. Stanley would be your horny wife Jackie. It could be better, in which case maybe you don't need to read that draft ... I'll show you the next one.'

She did not look up from the page.

Some of you may remember the first page of this book, and those of you who don't (and I was one of those, as I stood across the table from my mum, trying to read it upside down, wondering what precisely it was I had said about her in the opening paragraphs) can flick back and see that it starts rather flatteringly about Susie. I went to get a cup of coffee and looked over her shoulder and saw the sentences about her and Stanley's arrival in France looking so handsome and sexy. I saw a smile play over her face. But I knew what was coming up. I was starting my retreat when I saw the smile slide from her features. She stopped reading and started flicking forward to random pages. I slowly backed out of the room. She picked up a pen, bracketed a paragraph and wrote *How could you?*

'I think I'll take a walk, leave you in peace,' I said and nipped downstairs, pulled my boots on and escaped outside.

The weather was crisp and clear. The village was silent, even by the standards of that place, and I stood alone in the cloistered square looking down the cobbles at the shuttered house where I used to live. The bar had closed for the winter. Without tourists Castelnau had turned from a Beryl Cook into a Utrillo. There weren't even any council workers on a cigarette break, though I did smell the tang of wood smoke hanging sharply in the air from where someone at the bottom of a chimney sat huddled around a fireplace waiting for May.

I walked down the slope, past a gite where the pool furniture had been stacked hurriedly in the lean-to, and the swimming pool winterised. I strode between white fields of frosted stalks. Under the bare branches of an oak I walked over the leaves that in the summer I had walked under. Stopping on a metal bridge and looking at the river, in no mad rush to get back, I thought *that's not a river, it's agricultural run-off.* The reflection of the branches trembled on the inert water. I could see the farmer, busy grubbing up a hedge in a brand new digger. Further down the deserted road a farmhouse dog ran up and down a length of slack electric tape.

I wondered whether turning this book into a work of fiction would reduce its impact. Of course you might suspect that I have already done that, and that Susie is the fictional version of someone else altogether, or that she is a product of my imagination. But she is not. Oh that she were. It would have made the walk back up to the fortress village a whole lot easier.

Susie had moved into her study. I put my head round the door. She lifted the manuscript and said 'This is going to cost you 5 per cent. Plus you're going to have write me some jokes for my powerboat book.'

I said, 'Well I think I owe you some to be honest, so count me in.'

As I pulled my jumper over my head in the spare room I thought *maybe this isn't going to be too bad after all.*

Since my last visit, Stanley had visibly slowed, and his speech was now pretty unintelligible to anyone who wasn't a fluent Stanley speaker. 'Wooouuyooo merry dear fixing a wha?' meant *Can I have a whisky.* He remained in his studio, glued not to his models but to the screen, looking at financial charts.

'I never knew that I went on so much,' Susie said to me in the kitchen.

'Well you don't always,' I said. 'I am a bit of an exaggerator,' I added.

She raised an eyebrow.

'I felt REALLY bad when I read some of your descriptions of me,' she said.

'Well we all have annoying habits, me more than you,' I said. 'And I make stuff up all the time. It's the only defence I have against reality.'

'We'll talk when I've finished reading it,' she said, returning to her office.

She emerged at about 7pm, by which time I was fortified by a bottle or two of wine. Things were made severely worse by the fact that she was on antibiotics and not allowed alcohol.

I asked 'Can I ask you to contribute 2000 words to the book, as it invites you to in the text? Or should I novelise it? Remove you from it entirely? I have had a think about it and believe the text would work as a novel.'

'I will write the 2000 words,' she said 'if you don't change them.'

'Of course,' I said.

She snorted dismissively.

'I will give you full editorial control over your words,' I said.

Castelnau was so quiet that when I woke up in the dead of the night I could hear my mother tapping at her keyboard in the room below.

In the morning she said 'I love writing.'

'Is that your chapter you are doing?' I asked.

'Oh yes,' she said, almost triumphantly.

'Remember,' I said. 'What the reader wants to know is what is in your mind vis-à-vis the subject of your death. Maybe touch on the difference between holding these views in theory and carrying them out in practice. They want to know if you are still planning on killing yourself, and if so, what are you waiting for? What are the conditions that have to be met for you to do it? Those kinds of things.'

She smiled at me.

I said 'I don't think the reader is interested in a ding-dong battle between you and me.'

'Bit late to say that,' she said.

That sounded grim. She was up late again the next night, tapping away, and seemed worryingly flushed with success in the morning.

'I have been thinking again of turning it into a novel,' I said. 'Easier …'

'No,' she said. 'I feel far too strongly about it now. This is going to be my last campaign.'

'So you aren't going to do, er, *it*, before this book comes out?' I had long thought, as I am sure you have, that it would make the obvious, crowd-pleasing end. And that I was therefore going to have to wait for her death before finishing the book.

'Certainly not. I want to be on hand to publicise it, for a start. Do you actually have a publisher? If you don't, maybe I could help you. My connections are better than yours. And it is *our* book, after all.'

Yes. I heard that too.

I didn't want to rain on her parade as she still had to hand in her chapter and I needed to keep her sweet. But over the next forty-eight hours I sensed the steering wheel of this book being wrenched from my hands, making the manuscript slew frighteningly across the road into the oncoming traffic of another one of Susie's campaigns, which meant I was likely to be left upside down in the wreckage.

I decided that the sooner I finished the book the better it would be. There was absolutely no point waiting for Susie to Sign Out now the prospect of a good 10-minute slot on *Woman's Hour* running rings round Jane Garvey was on the cards. I could see her imagining the attention she might get if the book was a success. For a good few weeks she would fill the features pages and bestride the airwaves, holding forth. And knowing Susie, she would inevitably cook up a lawsuit. Get the war room back up and running. I had read of scores of accounts of people petitioning courts to let them die by their own hand. That would be irresistible to her. Kennaway vs Thomson and Another would be joined on the statute books by Kennaway vs The Rest of the World and Another.

When telling my French film-director friend about this book, he had said 'Oh, that sounds like an interesting movie'. So it looked like, far from waving goodbye to my mother in a dignified, honest and heart-wrenching final year, the whole project had badly backfired and I was now being forced to join a campaign with her, and possibly have a movie made about her, all of which would take years. I really couldn't see her missing out on that. And in the million-to-one chance that all this came to pass I realised that I would have to reconsider my firm opinion at the start of this book, which was meant to be, after all, about my mum's death, that there was absolutely no way there could ever be a sequel. Now I was staring at the prospect of Season 2 of the box set with my mum as co-producer.

So, my friend and companion, every time you recommend this book, you almost certainly extend Susie's life. In that case, I have to admit, we have accomplished something.

'I am writing notes on your manuscript,' she said.

I knew that. I had sneaked a look while she was cooking a three-course meal for Stanley, as she did every lunch and dinner. She seemed to have quite a lot to say, and from the intensity of the handwriting, was exercised about it. But she was friendly and kind over dinner and I had to admire what a good sport she was.

The next day I departed for Britain, and she hadn't finished making her notes. We agreed that she would send me both the annotated manuscript 'fact checked' by her, and her chapter. Before I left, she placed a card on the table.

'I thought you should know some of the things I have achieved in my life, almost none of which you have seen fit to mention. I have made a list.'

I reproduce Susie's list in full here. My notes are in italics:

Kenya

Boats (*court case*)

House – permission dealings (*she built a funky modernist house on a lake*)

Pinks – dealings (*her restaurant staffed only by women*)

Russia (*she organised a sit-in at the airport when a flight was cancelled*)

(China) (*holiday; not sure what it's doing on the list*)

RAF tattoo

CND

USAF

Upper Thames (*a conservation society that did its best to protect the higher reaches of the Thames from the ambitions of motorboat owners*)

Glous Trust (*wildlife protection*)

Passport for Pets (*she was active in the campaign to prevent dogs and cats being quarantined unnecessarily*)

Espoir phu san (*a charity she worked for to raise money for Vietnamese children, I never worked out why*)

*garden (*I love the asterisk*)

Small world practical action (*more charity, not sure quite what it was about*)

Batiment de France (*planning battle over her house restoration in Castelnau*)

Trees (*felling of*)

Selling the house (*slightly scraping the barrel here*)

China restoration (*I put my hand up on this one. It would have been right to mention that she was a skilled restorer of broken china*)

YDS (*her memoir* Yellow Duster Sisters, *published by Bloomsbury. You have to read it.*)

Pain/pills

Interesting that Kenya came first. Some weeks later, she mailed me her chapter.

Here, now, are her words …

TWENTY EIGHT

Killing oneself successfully is not something one can practise

I have decided not to obtain an injunction against Guy and this book. Obviously I could bring a successful action against him for defamation, slander and probably identity theft so ridiculously inaccurate is his portrayal of me and dear Stanley. Stanley has been pitilessly characterised as a comic drunk and a bit of an idiot, shuffling along in bedroom slippers. Damn it, he is 90 years old. A true picture of him could be just as amusing, but Guy seems to prefer cheap shots. His trouble is he can't see a belt without hitting below it.

I am confident that anyone reading this book will have well understood that the portrayal of my husband and me is a bizarre caricature.

It is a shame not to be taking Guy to court, for in a case as egregious as this, a custodial sentence would certainly be appropriate. I would enjoy sending him bad reviews of TIME TO GO *in prison. But jailing Guy for his cruelty and idiocy, though tempting, is not the priority here.*

Instead, I will just say F... you, Guy, and continue to the main point.

This book was to open up the question of dying and in particular my own pre-planned affair and possibly that of others'. Indeed I am old, well only 87, and do bear the bruises that always go with longevity, but nevertheless possess a mind.

I am a woman who stood up against the things that I considered to be wrong, sometimes a perceived injustice and sometimes a very real one. I used to think these things happened because I was a woman and because when James, my first husband, died, I was on my own. I really had to fight hard to achieve even very small things. My life soon became full of endeavours of every sort, sometimes so that I should not have too much time to think.

In this case it is so utterly reasonable, that which I want.

I am simply wanting to go while the going is still good, when I can be responsible for my life and my death. There is such an ugliness to old age, infirmity, incontinence, wiping and washing, loss of memory, dependency, lack of intimacy, failing eyesight, hearing, thinning hair and bossy nurses removing all the gin bottles from under our beds. And the tonic and lemon.

I have read constantly about suicides, but the public is rarely told of the means by which these are achieved. Like a good Girl Guide I realised that I had to be prepared for any event. There would be no time to start ordering pills on Google when the ambulance was on its way to take my broken body to an asylum for the insane.

Why the hell should anyone tell me I do not have the right to dispose of myself when and how I wish? I do not believe in God and in the same way I do not think that MPs, Lords, the judiciary and the Church (and according to Archbishop Welby only 15 per cent of the British people are considered to be true Christians) should be permitted to arbitrate on my death. How did we get here? Why shackle doctors with an oath conceived centuries ago that now does not carry much relevance? In the light of the progress medicine has made today, keeping a lot of us alive for far too long with a rotten quality of everyday living is senseless. Why should they be fettered from doing what any human would wish to do for someone longing to quit? Is it beautiful, laudable and good to keep someone alive in crucial pain, or semi-conscious on the end of a feeding drip, morphine or an oxygen mask?

And here I am not just speaking of illness and pain as a reason for death. I am talking about the time to live and the time to die. I am asking on behalf of those of us who have lived fine lives and do not want to end up in a care home, no longer in charge of making decisions for ourselves. It is quite enough to have to cope with the fight against growing incapacity. (In my case arthritis and an inability to walk properly), without having a stranger dictate to me how to manage my release. We could all too easily decide to take the decision long before strictly necessary, just in case we might not be capable of organising casting-off while drowning in a storm. My choice. Our choice.

Is anyone there who really cares? Is it a good idea to force us to make what might be a bosh shot with a DIY kit? After all, killing oneself successfully is not something one can practise. Does anyone really believe that giving help to a person looking for a decent exit is an unkind move? Or evil? Do they begin to understand our predicament? Is it that they follow the Bible? They should cast a glance at the Book of Leviticus. Oh dearie me, the Bible says that I can sell my daughter into slavery, but by careless oversight forgets to tell me how much silver I should ask for her. Or is it some even more ancient belief, that to end your own life is a sin? Tell me why I should be a victim of a bunch of pious people who do not know me, or me them, people who perhaps have not given quite enough thought to their decisions concerning pain and grief and desperation. Why do they have the right to dictate to me or to punish anyone else who does decide to manage their own death or help them to their end?

We have, most of us, moved on in so many matters: homosexuality, women's rights, education, science, crimes against humanity, genocides, and abortion (I could go on), but why not move on with this?

They argue a planned death might – I say might – encourage perhaps, a family to take a path to hasten the death of a relative in order to benefit themselves in some way – possibly for cash reasons or maybe even the repossession of a house. If those MPs who debate this subject cannot even provide enough houses and hospitals for the country, how the hell may they be allowed to pontificate on death? I would argue that most people know and understand exactly what they are doing when making their plans. And I ask indeed precisely how many families would be able to take a pecuniary advantage of their relatives in comparison to the number of people who want to quit dependency and pain?

A discrete and private consultation with a provider of drugs could help. But that is currently utterly unlikely, and while a trawl across the Internet might more easily yield some interesting information if you could only trust it, a simple plastic bag could do the trick but is horrendous to contemplate. It comes to something when I have to start sizing up precipitous roads (lots round here) while contemplating Thelma and Louise.

A wish for justice has been, I now realise, a big motivator in my life; I was a mouse in my early years. It was only on the death of my first husband, when he was 40, leaving me a clueless widow at 38, and his four children, that I woke up to realise that if some-thing needed to be done, I had to do it myself. No one else was about to help.

I always had a project ahead of me and when that stops I want to stop too. Campaigning and organising has been the blessing of my life and I have learnt so much. I cannot envisage waking up to a day without at least a bit of a cause, or something needing to be done. But this is not about me. This is very much about another new campaign. A fight, I might say, to the death and for the death.

I have succeeded in pulling the strings of life together through sheer persistence, and I am not prepared to give up now. Like a dog I cannot give up a bone. I have spent a great life, winning most of the way. But my wish now is to go out at the top, dying as I myself will plan – but if it is the least bit of comfort to anyone I can assure you the moment has not arrived.

What am I waiting for? I need time to look through the all the photographs that reflect a wonderful life, to finish mending a couple of things, to plan the planting of the terrace for next year, to order paints and varnishes and glue so that I can give my grandson's girlfriend some lessons in china restoration, and to write another book. So I can promise you, not just yet.

Only when I feel no more relish for life and its challenges will I enter the final straight. But it needs to be organised in advance. It really is an important subject, and as my aunt used to say, so often, if you want a job done properly, then you must do it yourself. But most people do not have the means or the knowledge.

Discussing various thoughts on death, and the way to achieve success when the time comes was spurred on by the thoughts of the growing incapacity of my cherished husband, and understanding that maybe I was not going to be strong enough to look after him myself. Then damn and blast it, with my own dodgy health, it might turn out to be the other way round. All too complicated. To dream of a mutually timed decease was, of course, totally impractical, though one does read in the papers, from time to time, that a happy old couple have success in dying together. But tell me how. Stanley and I held a comforting fantasy, one about which we needed to argue and play games and think of hilarious situations, in order to take our minds off the dreaded reality of one of us being left alone.

However, Guy's book has proved to me that I definitely have yet another challenging campaign ahead with which to tussle. I am ready for the fight. Even if it means combining forces and co-operating with my vexatious and ill-mannered son.

Justice for all says Chairman Susie.

TWENTY NINE

Susie's Law

WELL, I CAN'T SAY I DIDN'T have it coming. I hope you lot enjoyed that. Brace yourselves for her campaign. The phrase that stood out for me was: *Why do they have the right to dictate to me or to punish anyone else who does decide to manage their own death or help them to their end?* If her campaign gathers speed, as others have usually done, I look forward to a debate between a politician and my mother in which the politician claims this right over Susie. I would like to see that. He will be added I have no doubt to the long line of men, begun by the maitre d' at the Ngorongoro Crater Hotel, who tried to deny Susie her rights.

And choosing how you die is nothing less than a human right. It's just not acknowledged as one, the way the right to an education, or to free speech or to choosing your gender weren't acknowledged in the past. But it surely will be soon. The law is hopelessly inadequate for the times we live in, and it certainly will be changed. Those holding out against reform are sounding increasingly cranky and out of touch. The only question that remains in my mind is will it be called *Susie's Law* when it finally makes it onto the statute book?

Let me indulge in some predictions. By 2030 departure celebrations will be commonplace and, like weddings and funerals now, come in a wide variety of sizes and styles. Some will be sanctioned by religion. But probably not all. These ceremonies will be an opportunity for the dying to make a final statement, to draw a conclusion, to type themselves the full stop, or the exclamation mark, or even the question mark, on the sentence that started with their birth. Their life sentence. They will write their own end, rather than leave it to mainly disinterested strangers who dash it off for money.

By 2031 there will be departure-party planners, who will help you find a venue of your choice, provide the death doula, decor and ceremony that suits you. Some will be extravagant affairs with hundreds of relatives and friends, and others will be intimate goodbyes. It will be Instagrammed and Facebooked, or whatever it is then. By 2032 designated departure venues will have sprung up across the country, where your guests can drink and enjoy barbecued food before, during or after the event. By then we will have come a long way from the shameful trip to a Zurich suburb to die quietly behind heavy net curtains. Like everything else – assisted suicide will come out of the closet. You will be spammed about whether or not you have made the right kind of arrangements. ARE YOU LEAVING

IN STYLE? The service providers will ask. And of course it will be called *curating* your death, so your life has a standout design. It will be like finding the right couplet to attach to the end of a sonnet. It will complete your life. At the moment we are seeing people with 27-line sonnets, the final four of which are unintelligible drivel.

When they reissued Daid Bowie's album *Hunky Dory* on CD twenty years after the original vinyl release, it had mysteriously increased in length by three extra 'bonus' tracks. On listening, it turned out they weren't bonus, but rejects, and didn't add anything extra to the perfectly formed album that was *Hunky Dory* except unnecessary length that spoilt the compact shape of the original. That's what we do to our own lives with the final redundant years.

THIRTY

A bit dicky

I HAD HEARD THE NEWS that Stanley was ill, though not from Susie, who didn't like to make what she called a fuss. The truth had emerged during a visit by my sister Jane, who had arrived to find our mother struggling to look after a sick patient all by herself. *Least said soonest mended* is not an adage for the age we live in, but one that Susie swore by. It was particularly ineffective in the case of a 90-year-old man with a urinary tract infection.

Susie had called the doctor. When the result of what are now known as bloods, which always made me think of gang members, came through, it was clear the situation was critical. An ambulance was called and Stanley was ordered immediately to go to hospital. He refused to leave the house. He was urged by the doctor to go. He clearly stated that he would not.

Tough call. I was struck by the bravery of it.

He must have known what refusing hospital meant. But he wasn't on for an extended tussle with the infection in an alien institution. His English wasn't up to much, forget his French. He was going to take his chances at home. When I heard he had sent the ambulance away empty, I thought: I want to go and say goodbye to Stanley, and to thank him for being him.

I was at that time on the other side of the world, so I booked a flight back to Europe. Waiting to board, I spoke to Susie.

'He started crying this afternoon,' she said. 'And he said "I've just realised I'm not going to get better." He's realised he's going to die.'

As I bent an arc around the globe, I felt like talking to someone about my destination, but the person beside me, who had eaten his dinner starting with the cake and ending with the salad, the chocolate and a lick of the vinaigrette pot, didn't seem the right guy. When he went to sleep I thought of you. You, who have become my friend and confidant. You, who have heard all my conversations and thoughts about the time to go. I wrote those sentences in a pool of light in the dark cabin at 30,000 feet. How lonely death made me feel. May I take this opportunity to thank you for being such a good listener? You strengthen, encourage and help me. Out of the oval window was the void, the blackness that I feared so much. Stay close please, in my time of need. Don't desert me, by flicking forward to see where this ends; I have no idea and I have to stay here.

When we touched down at Gatwick, my phone, which I had accidentally left on, started pinging. Passengers shrugged, past caring that I had, according to air safety regulations, imperilled 375 people's lives including their own. I had a message from France: from now on it was palliative care only. Susie added: *could you please pick up a large pot of Sudocrem at the chemist for Stanley's skin? Don't ever let this happen to me.*

In the hall of the house in Castelnau there was a folded hospital bed with coiled power lead. I glanced at it from the staircase and thought how little its curved handrails and grey padded plastic gladdened the heart. Stanley's jovial son Rupert was upstairs. He had come, I guessed, on a similar mission to my own.

'Hello Guy,' he smiled. 'Great to see you. Welcome to Emergency Ward 10.'

Rupert's arrival, I was informed, had given Stanley a lift.

'That's good. Maybe he'll pull through,' I said.

'We will see,' Susie said to me, adding 'Death choses its own agenda,' an opinion entirely at variance with her stated philosophy.

Rupert and my sister Jane were in control of treatment, and decided which visitors were admitted. I was asked to stay downstairs, and spent an hour or two in the kitchen watching the tag team of professional nurses come and go while my sister made some tiny meals and took them up on a tray.

Jane and Rupert wanted Stanley to look his best when he saw me. We three didn't often meet, but with Stanley and Mum in the house it felt more like a family than it had in years. There were no longer weddings to meet up at, so now only death brought us together.

'People are ringing up,' Jane said to me. 'Old friends. Even people who didn't particularly know him. They're all trying to see him. When I tell them he's not up to seeing anyone they say *Oh I just want to pop my head round the door* or *I just want to give him a quick hug*. He doesn't want to be seen like that. You're at your absolute lowest ebb and people want to come and stare at you. Honestly!'

I could see how a good farewell was important. On the threshold of death people possess new powers of judgement. An acquaintance of mine who was dying of cancer seemed to get popular in her final month. I wanted to be one of her visitors. If Stanley's callers were anything like me, they wanted it to be cool with him before he died. I had perhaps not treated my friend as well as I could have in the past. It was as though she had the ability to take news forward from here into the next place. I didn't want her ruining my reputation in the afterlife. It was bad enough in this one. I wanted the souls who were dead, wherever they were, to like me, or, failing that, at least never to have heard of me before I could show up and start with the excuses. I suspected that we who wanted to see my friend also thought that we could resolve something with her. We wanted to sit by her bed, be nice, and feel shit about her bad luck and our good.

Later Jane said 'Go easy, Guy, this isn't the time for jokes.'

I duly fell into hospital mode: lowering my voice, careful not to make any unnecessary noises, speaking in a hushed, earnest manner, and cutting the gags out. But I felt fake. I was sensitivity signalling. But I did it for my sister and mother.

Rupert didn't do my bullshit sensitivity. He dealt with the pain head on with laughter. He trotted down the stairs roaring his head off. 'I've done some things in my life, Guy,' he shouted, 'but I never thought I'd clean the old man's todger!' He laughed again. 'That's a first, I can tell you. Ruddy hell.'

I was ushered upstairs; outside the bedroom door were some sinister hospital appliances. One was a machine to stand a patient up. The other ... I never discovered its use.

Then suddenly I was in the large light-filled room with the endless countryside in four big windows, looking at Stanley, in a high hospital bed, a handle dangling over him like a noose. Since I last saw him, only a few months ago, he had lost all remaining weight. He turned his head and fixed me with huge eyes. His mouth opened, closed and opened again.

Then he croaked 'Siiindoooo her um.' Deep Stanley, this was. Patois Stanley.

I looked at my mum, a native speaker. 'He says it is so kind of you to come,' she said.

'I wouldn't miss it for anything,' I said. I looked at the drip at the end of the bed with its tube that disappeared under the blanket. There was another tube snaking out of the bed into a bag in a blue bucket. In and out. He lay back and closed his eyes. His hands moved under the blanket.

'He's not tossing himself off is he?' Rupert said. 'He asked one of the nurses if she wanted a shag. Utterly hilarious. I told her that he was a little confused but looking at her I thought he was spot on.'

I was expecting Stanley and the room to smell of decay, of death I suppose, but only picked up a hint of soap. I sat watching him, wondering what to do and say.

His eyes opened. 'How are yoooo?' he fluted.

'I'm fine.' I very nearly did what I usually did with ill people, which was to start complaining about my own health. But I stopped myself. I had a little speech prepared saying that I loved him, and wanted to thank him for being such a great stepfather, but since the news of his improving condition, thought it might strike the wrong tone.

'I really just came to say hello,' I said.

'Whaa? All the waaayfra Jamaica?' he said.

'It does sound odd, I agree,' I smiled. I took his hand and squeezed it. 'I am glad I am here,' I said. 'Good to see you.' I sat with him for half an hour before I leant forward and said 'I love you.'

He nodded slowly and his eyes filled with tears.

Later I helped him find the *Financial Times* on his tablet. The screen asked me for his password. I looked at him with his head tilted back, his knees like coat hangers and his eyes rolling around and thought, this is a long shot.

'Can you remember your password?' I asked.

'Yes,' he said, and smiled serenely. 'I – R – E – N – E – V' he said. His mother's name and the first letter of her surname. I typed it and it worked. I passed him back the tablet. 'Than you,' he said.

After looking at the newspaper for a few minutes he said something so extraordinary about the economy I wrote it down on a scrap of cardboard torn from a packet of pills and stuffed it in my pocket so I wouldn't forget it.

He told me he wanted a sleep, so I stood up and said 'goodbye.' I wasn't quite sure what tone to use as I didn't know if it was for a few hours or forever.

It turned out that it was forever. The next day there was a change. He was ill again. But it wasn't to be a smooth glide into a velvet cloak.

I was downstairs in the engine room and caught snatches of conversation:

He's having trouble talking.
The bedsores are bad today.
He's slipping down the bed.
He got tangled in sheets in the night and pulled out one of his tubes and made a mess.

People pushed past me with urgency. I knew he was having trouble swallowing. A spoonful of water made him cough and cough and cough. I heard the retching and heaving as the bedroom door opened and closed on the floor above.

When I was admitted later he seemed unconscious. He lay back with his mouth open and dry. It had about its rim a touch of Francis Bacon. His breathing was sterterous, steady and deep. I was expecting it to be shallow and uneven.

I sat watching him. Occasionally his body would twitch, a finger flex. It was like there was someone going round the house of Stanley turning out the lights. The circuits had been a bit dicky for some time. Do you remember the May/Snow short circuit? In the grassy ruins of Stanley's mind, the janitor was closing the car park and switching off the floodlights. The man was dying.

I watched the people around him go about the grinding work of what is called caring. He was a huge baby, but losing, not gaining, weight, perception and reactions every hour. I left the room for the nappy change but came back in a touch early and glimpsed the shiny skeletal limbs that Jane and a nurse were gently rubbing with cream before a blanket was drawn over them.

Jane, Rupert and Susie's lives were entirely on hold. Jane particularly had been working punishingly long hours, and was up and down all night. Feeding took hours because the slightest thing made him retch and cough. They had already been at it for a week before I turned up, and I was whacked after just watching it for 48 hours. Nothing else went on in that house. There was no other subject of conversation, no other event, apart from Stanley and his health, and this crawl to death. It seemed that the lives of the carers were entirely ignored. They were expected to continue to service Stanley without complaint. Their quality of life, or let's face it poor old Stanley's, was not permitted to be questioned.

Everyone was losing the will to live, except Stanley.

I thought I was to witness a gentle drift into the open arms of a sweet death, but somehow it had turned into a desperate last ditch operation to keep him alive for another few hours, traumatising us all.

THIRTY ONE

The moment was perfect

T HAT NIGHT WAS PREDICTED to be his last. Again. But he was still there in the morning, looking a bit more lost and bewildered, unable to talk. The carers went about their work, jolly and exhausted. The nurses changed the colostomy bag by the bed as though it were a lark. My mum, poor woman, had taken delivery of some berberis plants which were to replace the two (now) stolen, and had accidentally poked herself between her eyes with one of their points. She had of course read all I had written about her and the berberis, and now possessed the grace and humour to have a good laugh with me about her bruise. She spent her time, when not staring at Stanley, cleaning out the fridge and doing housework in the kitchen. I could see she missed cooking for him.

In the afternoon I was with Stanley when Susie came into their room. At night she touchingly still slept in the bed next to him. I was sitting in the bucket chair I had been in when a year ago Susie had told me about her plan to control the manner and time of her and Stanley's deaths. Stanley was now restless and uncomfortable, occasionally garbling something incomprehensible. He was going to die and he was somewhere I'd put between the outskirts of that sprawling suburb Discomfort near the dual carriageway to the ancient city of Agony. What they call a bad place.

Here was precisely the situation that I and my mother had talked about, almost trained for. The nurse tag team were at another house, my sister sleeping, Rupert on the phone to his wife, soaking up a bollocking; the moment was perfect. Looking after Stanley after she died had been her last impediment to killing herself, she had told me, and that obligation was about to stop.

But what to do? I had earlier found out, with some dismay, that Stanley was still on a course of antibiotics. And I had been told we were on palliative care only. And it wasn't like Jane or Rupert or Susie could quietly forget to give the antibiotic pills to him; the tag team delivered them under somebody's orders, I never quite knew whose, by shots, so there was no stopping that. It was though the ordeal had to be drawn out. Even when poor old Stanley was dead I imagined the nurses dragging his body out of the fridge in the morgue and in their relentlessly upbeat manner ramming antibiotics into his corpse on 40 euros an hour, plus the drugs.

I had noticed – and been astonished by – the amount of medical supplies in his room. Two large tables were entirely taken up with his needs. I say his needs, but who knew what they were? I was more inclined to think it was the needs of the pharmaceutical company that were being met first, with all these drugs, pads, dressings, unguents, ointments, creams, applicators, drip bags and other to me unidentifiable heavily packaged medical gizmos. The drug company of course also sold the antibiotics that – although we agreed he wouldn't have – were nevertheless *still* being injected into him. I began to see what a scam keeping Stanley alive was for the pharmaceutical industry. I already loathed the drug companies on grounds of their packaging and their adoration of single-use plastics. Why use a glass bottle or cardboard box as a recyclable receptacle when you can spread 8 pills into three blister packs of plastic and put them into two plastic coated cartons? Every day I saw a flip-top bin of medical waste being poured into the garbage downstairs.

I looked at Stanley. It wouldn't take much. A pillow on his face. Softly would do it. With care, attention, and love. But what if his spindly hands tried to peel mine off? I would have to sit back down and pretend I hadn't been trying to kill him. Which would be slightly embarrassing. And later, if he came to, meet his wounded gaze. I wondered about holding the in-tube in a tight bend out of his sight but didn't know how long it would take to work.

Susie stood up and pointed at the door.

'You must leave now,' she calmly said.

'Of course.' I assumed she was going to lie on her bed for a siesta, but when I got outside and noticed that the door, after being shut, had opened a crack, something made me softly step back towards it and look into the room. Susie's back was to me as she looked in a drawer. She turned, holding a small silver box, biting her lip, looking worried. She opened the box and took out two white capsules, slowly sitting on Stanley's bed. She kissed his cheek and opened one of the capsules into his upturned mouth, reaching for a glass of water and giving him a sip to wash it down. Then she put the other in her mouth, took a long drink of water, set the glass carefully on the bedside table, and sat back beside Stanley, holding his hand with her eyes closed. Then I saw her smile.

Or at least … that is what would have happened if we'd gone the novelisation route. But we are stuck in non-fiction land here, the place that makes the rules, and she didn't usher me out of the room.

We both sat there, possibly thinking the same thing: this is the moment. But doing nothing. Then the moment passed. We said nothing. We watched his pain in ours. Susie did later tell me that she too had thoughts of smothering him.

'The next day, there were long strings of a gluey mucus type substance coming from his open mouth,' she said to me. 'Which I pulled with my fingers, on and on until it broke, but I knew that there was a lot more from where that came. I had a big towel in my hand and I wanted to end the agony and then I asked myself, frightened to hell, what I would do if he attempted to struggle? I put away the towel and cried, for him and for me.'

I also didn't want to kill him because it just didn't seem right, lame as that sounds after everything I have said in this book, even in the state he was in. I guess I didn't know if he was trying to die or trying to stay alive. He seemed crap at both. Was it him, or them, keeping him going? I couldn't tell, though he had said no to going to hospital, which was a bit of a hint. But then – maybe – he'd looked down the riveted bulge of the ferry into the veined water and thought *I'm not doing that either.*

What we needed, all three of us, I suspected, was someone to do it for us. In the old days, before antibiotics, drips and in- and out-pipes, the robed priest, with a few Latin phrases, bible and crucifix could be relied on to tip people over the edge. Extreme Unction. But Stanley was too strong. I remembered what Amanda had said to Nanna (who, incidentally, was still going great guns in the care home in Nottingham): *You are free to go.*

Although I liked that phrase, I didn't feel it was my place to use it, and to be honest I don't think Stanley could be shuffled off his mortal coil with mere words.

We needed extreme, extreme unction. A lay priest, or celebrant, who provided the whole package. Someone who would arrive at the house, bidden (or maybe called by some magic instinct), bringing dignity, tenderness and beauty to the proceedings, spreading calm with his humble presence. Actually, it could easily be a her. In fact probably better if it was. A reverse doula, helping the soul out of life, not into it. She was definitely nothing to do with big pharma – she came not from the chemist but from nature, and walked barefoot wearing a garland of ivy and wild garlic, holding a basket of herbs and plants. She would spend time looking at and talking to Stanley. Then, with a wise smile take from her basket … a beaker of easeful death. A sweet-tasting mixture laced with opium, hemlock and deadly nightshade, all timed to go off in the most painless but effective sequence. The job would be done. By tradition she would be paid only with food and wine.

But that didn't happen either, and we were, not to put too fine a point on it, stuck with Stanley for yet another traumatic and grisly night.

Late in the afternoon, Jane, having a drink at the kitchen island, said to me, '74, Guy. That's the best age to die. I've seen 'em go at all ages, and 74 is optimum. That's the tops, that's what I am aiming for.'

'That gives me 14 years,' I said.

'It makes you use them,' she said.

'I can imagine that,' I replied.

My sister was suggesting the curated life. A life with a sealed rather than frayed end. A sonnet with 14 lines, rather than 27.

Later Jane said 'I don't think he's going any time too soon. Why don't you take Mummy out to dinner?'

THIRTY TWO

The last sentence of silence

I BOOKED A TABLE AND Susie wrapped herself in a cashmere shawl for the outing. I noticed that without Stanley my mum moved like a hare. I had to catch her up at the door of the restaurant. The waitress double-checked my order for two coupes of champagne and a bottle of wine. I explained it was correct; we were English.

I asked Susie if it was all reminding her of my father's death. She said something and then stopped. She waved at her neck.

'That's not emotion, it's my throat,' she said, taking a sip of water. 'I don't remember much about your father's funeral.'

Nor did I. I was eleven years old. I only recalled standing in a pew in an English country church and suddenly being aware of a pale coffin on a sinister, large wheeled conveyance sliding into view and resting motionless in the aisle. And I thought, my dad's in that box.

'What I remember the most,' Susie said, putting down her glass of water, 'after getting out of the car at the church – I don't remember who made any of the arrangements – was seeing this, I think it's called a gurney, with big wheels, with the coffin on it. That thing has stuck in my mind.'

'Yes, it had big wheels,' I said, 'with long spokes, I suppose for getting up church steps and along bumpy medieval paths. It was spooky.'

'Mmm,' we both said.

As a child I had pictured my father inside the coffin, his hands crossed over his shroud. In his mouth was a scuba-diving regulator, and beside him an oxygen cylinder. He had just enough air to get him through the service and into the grave. As soon as the congregation had left the churchyard, the grave-diggers lifted the coffin, forced the lid, and gave my father a hand up. He pulled out the mouth-piece and tugged off his shroud to reveal a dinner jacket and bow tie. This was clearly the influence of *You Only Live Twice* on the imagination of a frightened and lonely little boy. The movie was released in 1967 and my father died in '68. Standing beside the coffin my father struck a Bond-like pose. In real life he was fairly James Bondian, particularly in the Connery manifestation. Handsome, intense, glamorous, and smouldering with sex and danger. He sniffed the air, slid a silver cigarette case from his breast pocket, lit a Senior Service, snapped it shut, exhaled and said 'Thank you gentlemen, mission accomplished. I'd better go and see M. But first I need to pay a visit to Pussy. She'll be wanting a full debrief.' He strode under the lynch gate to the curb, where a man pulled a tarpaulin off the white roadster we thought he had died in. He climbed in and accelerated over the horizon. Leaving us lot behind to battle on.

During one of my last shifts at Stanley's bedside I had noticed a copy of *Silence* on the bookshelf under the window. I mentioned that when my father died they found – in his top pocket – a piece of paper with the last sentence of the novel written on it. I opened the slim book as Stanley slept, and read it.

There followed a bloody accusing confusion and crying noise.

No kidding.

My father, who knew a thing or two about life and death, carried his last sentence on him. He knew that you had to write, and live, to a full stop, rather than peter out in an endless chain of increasingly meaningless words that ramble and drivel and repeat and ramble and drivel until finally running out of gas before starting up again but even more weakly and never quite getting to a satisfactory end …

You get the picture.

The pain that existed within me was so patient. It would not leave until I gave it the wholehearted attention it demanded. All I did by ignoring it was pass it around my closest friends, family and down to my children.

Turning away from death, or rather trying to laugh in its face, had not served me particularly well. My progress through life had been like a game of emotional Takeshi's Castle, the details of which are tedious to the outsider, and depressing to the insider. I stumbled and slipped and slid on and off a colourful range of self-destructive behaviours which other people seemed to land on and alight from with ease. When I stopped to catch my breath and gather myself I looked up and was hit in the face by the next stupid thing I did, and sent slapping into the water for another dousing. The best I had hoped for was to give a few people some entertainment along the way.

I looked at my mum's soft creased face. Forty-nine years had passed since the funeral, but we had not talked of it until then. The pain of that day had been piled upon more pain, the fear on confusion, and all had been compacted so tightly it seemed overwhelmingly difficult to go back through to separate the sedimentary layers. My father's death, and its strange silent aftermath, had never been faced. I do not think I had even once spoken to my brother about it. But Susie and I glimpsed it there for a moment, when the door opened briefly on that day.

I had noticed that I had recently felt the pain of simply being Guy easing. My long drives through France, for instance, or living by myself in the village, had been scary and lonely undertakings in the past. But I found myself now engaged in fewer elaborate acts of self-destruction, and that was a blessed relief. Was it because this process with Susie had cleared blocked lines of communication between me and her? Had she, like a good therapist, helped me reach back in time to turn the dial on the locked safe of who I am? I had spent many hours with counsellors trying to remember, or to guess, or to chance upon or to deduce, the combination that would make it click and the door swing open.

By facing death with my mother had I in some way corrected the fault with my father's that had caused so much trouble in my life? Was this the attention that my pain demanded, and that I was finally giving it? Who knew? Maybe I had just wised up, grown up and pulled myself together. It made dealing with Susie so much easier, and made living with this new person, me, so much more rewarding.

'How do you feel about your own death?' I asked, enjoying this new freedom I felt with her.

'I don't feel like doing it now, to myself,' she said. 'Because now I have a cause,' she smiled. 'But I absolutely refuse to go through what poor old Stanley is. I really don't want to end like that.'

'Nor do I.'

'And I shall fight for the right for none of us to be put through it against our will.'

The next day I left the house. Stanley was asleep or unconscious when I said goodbye, so it really didn't matter what tone I used. I left the carers there. That's a tough phrase. Their suffering was to continue to the end. Jane, my sister, was absolutely selfless in her service to Susie and Stanley.

On my way to Toulouse Airport I stopped for diesel because I didn't want the rental company to charge me an exorbitant sum to top up the tank. In the end they charged me 80 euros for bringing the car back over an hour early. Handling fee. I didn't think God would charge a handling fee for people returning early. I was just wondering how full I had to make the tank to get the needle on the French equivalent of F, when I saw a little single-seater plane flying over some leafless woods beyond the carriageway, which reminded me of the Sopwith Camel. I fancied it was Stanley at the controls.

'With his hand firmly on his joystick!' I imagined Rupert shouting. I pictured Stanley's windblown face and carefree smile.

I screwed the petrol cap on, and felt in my pockets for some French cash, as I didn't want to leave France with unspent coins and notes. In my hand I found the torn bit of packaging I had written Stanley's comment about the economy on.

It read: *It's the beginning of the end. There's going to be an enormous crash.*

Pretty good last words.

I drew over by the compressed air and texted the house for news. The reply came back. No news. He was still holding on.

THIRTY THREE

Stanley sitting on a shelf

S TANLEY WENT ON FOR another few grim days. My poor sister and mum had to endure it with the professional help. It harrowed them. When he did die, a stranger broke the news to me accidentally by email. She thought I knew. But I was absolutely not upset. I had already priced death into his valuation. I guess I have with everyone. It is going to happen to us all. I am going to lose even you, my companion. So let us live and laugh before we die.

As the news filtered out, so the messages of condolence fluttered in. My mum said she had 60 letters. People said on Facebook to me: *I am sorry for your loss* and added a heart emoji.

I typed: *I am truly happy Stanley has died. He is much better dead than alive. When I heard, I punched the air. He was a trapped animal that has finally escaped and run back into the wild.*

Then I deleted it, because I felt I had to fake grief the same way some people fake orgasm, to make others feel better, and to get it over with. There was a whiff of giving to charity in public. Charity signalling. Why signal anything? Be. There should be a story called 'The Boy Who Cried Grief'! And it should be read by all those people who in public overempathise and lard on the solemnity on the occasion of a death, though when in private never think again about the person. As fake laughter makes a thing less funny, so canned grief trivialises death. After a terrorist killed people outside a mosque, a friend from Somerset shared on FB: *Feeling completely heartbroken for Finsbury Park. Heart.* You are not completely heartbroken, I thought, as I read it. How could you lie about such an important thing? Faking grief is a disgrace. Like antibiotics, overuse renders grief ineffective. When we really need its power to convey our pain, all we can come up with is a bunch of clichés, like garage flowers, that can't begin to do justice to the majesty of the grim reaper or the mystery of the old man by the lake.

And it really was impossible to convey my happiness at Stanley's death.

ME: I am really pleased he died. He was ready. It was time.

SOMEONE: Of course, but it's sad. I am sorry.

It looked as though I were denying my sadness, but that wasn't the case. Since seeing Stanley on that hospital bed I didn't subscribe to the idea that you were alive until your heart stops beating. I was grieving not when my friend accidentally told me he had passed away, but when I saw Stanley stretched out in his own home, a dry husk with a gaping mouth. He was wounded and hurt, never to regain his power, unable to be himself any more, incapable of leaving on his own and forbidden to be helped out the door. That was when I grieved. Now he was dead he was Stanley again, in all his former glory. We could talk about his strengths and his foibles, his achievements and his failures. We could tell stories that delighted us and honoured him, bringing him alive amongst us. That was now our job, to acknowledge his abiding spirit with tales of his life.

I rang Susie. Jane took the phone and said 'I'm afraid she can't talk, she just bursts into tears.' My mother was in genuine grief. I respected and loved her for that.

They had a quiet funeral and cremation. Afterwards I received a short email from Susie:

Today was beautiful in its simplicity. He's home now and sitting on a shelf in his study between a bomber and a spitfire.

I didn't quite understand what she meant until I realised she was referring to his ashes, which must have been placed on a shelf by his model aeroplanes.

I wrote an obituary:

Stanley was born into a naval family but was unsuited to making war, preferring to make art and love. He became a successful show-business accountant, who did not drop the names of his famous clients. He had class like that.

He was already a loving father when he turned up at Mallam Waters in the 1980s, where he also became a kind and considerate step-father. He brought to the household an air of calm and harmony. He was happy, amusing, easy-going, creative, multi-skilled, and generous – though I have not yet seen the will. He was always up to something interesting, usually wearing a kaftan, with a large gin and tonic in his hand and a serene smile on his face. He painted pictures, developed and printed photographs, built sculptures, brewed cider and wine, grew beautiful vegetables and constructed incredibly complex scale models of ships and of aeroplanes, the latter which usually crashed on their maiden flight. These disasters Stanley always took with extraordinary equanimity considering how long he had taken to construct the doomed aircraft. The only thing Stanley really couldn't do was admit how talented he was.

He once explained that he called the theory behind his life 'positive drift', which basically meant interfering with things as little as possible, never complaining and enjoying all that existence on earth had to offer.

There remain two aspects of his life that cannot go unmentioned. The first is his collection he leaves behind of outrageous inappropriate remarks, on almost any subject, with which he could stun any social gathering. With Stanley's passing a fine example of old-school pre-political correctness has died. We will not hear remarks

236

like those again, at least not without criminal charges being brought. His other great achievement was his second marriage, to Susie, whom he loved unconditionally. It was a great union, full of creativity, adventures, laughter and joy. He always defended and protected Susie; indeed, one night, soon after they moved to France, he saw an unfamiliar car inching down the drive, so he picked up a shotgun, loaded it, and went outside, fearlessly, to challenge the intruders. After waving the gun at them and barking at them in English, no doubt, the occupants of the car finally got him to understand that they were neighbours bringing back the dog, which had got lost earlier in the day.

Now Stanley is up in heaven, where his days consist of long sessions at the modelling table, followed by a thorough perusal of the FT, before a gentle amble to the drinks cupboard and glance at the hob and a quick lift of a lid to see what Susie has made him for supper. Farewell Stanley. We will all see you again one of these days.

After the funeral Susie sprung into action. I wondered whether it was to blot out the fact that she had told me a month before that the only thing stopping her going to meet the old man by the lake was having to look after Stanley, an obstacle that no longer existed. Instead of killing herself, she had summoned the builders to remodel the house, and got busy dealing with the legal consequences of a death in

France. Apparently there is a *lot* of red tape. From the way she described it I couldn't understand why anyone in France bothered. We spoke on the phone about this book. She started to try and get me to remove some of the cheekier passages, and I said to her that if she wanted a portrait, I was her man, if she wanted an advert, she had to do it herself. She said she might just do that.

THIRTY FOUR

At a tin table

I T WAS SPRING WHEN I returned to France, but the wind rattling the shutters was still sharp. I sat outside Le Bar des Arcades and held my jacket around me. Tourists were trickling back to Castelnau; they looked like couples at the end of a relationship. They stood apart, staring at the buildings, bored, before hitting the bar, for a coffee. I thought, you won't mend your relationship at a tin table in George's sullen force field.

I took my usual walk down to the river, stopping to watch some worms wriggle onto the tarmac. They had seen what the farmers had done to the soil and had hung up the towel. They too had their red line. The mayor had been up to his old tricks and built a lavish new traffic calming scheme at the bottom of the hill, studding the medieval road with plastic bollards, zigzags, speed bumps and chicanes. There was a whiff of Toytown about it, and I kept thinking Noddy was about to hove into view, now an expat with his now openly gay lover Big Ears.

In a hedgeless field in the valley, a crop of peas was being sprayed with a fine mist of poison. I stood on the metal bridge and watched the river's surface plaiting like a Fair Isle sweater.

My mother was shaky and tired. I saw her asleep for the first time in decades, and was surprised she slept on her side. I thought she would sleep on her back, the quicker to leap into action, possibly with a weapon in her hand. At lunch she laid my plate at the end of the table, in Stanley's place. I sat in the chair he had used before the wheelchair. This made me think one thing: you're next chum.

She seemed only loosely moored in the present and often floated out onto the ocean of the past. I stood beside her as she went through old photograph albums, talking about events from its pages. She brought up my father a few times. When she gave me her bank card to get her cash at the ATM I noticed the pin code was 6868. He had died in 1968. Had the date been that much on her mind?

Twice she spoke about my father's car accident. She told me about a friend of his, a film director called Basil Dearden, who had died on the same spot of the M4, in a suicide, she claimed.

'You don't think it was in any way connected to Dad's accident?' I asked.

She nodded.

I thought, that seems ridiculously unlikely, but said nothing. Later I checked the date of Dearden's death: 1971. Dearden's *Wikipedia* entry did not even hint at suicide, but it did say he died on the M4, near Hillingdon. I never knew on which stretch of the motorway my father had met his barrier.

One evening Susie mentioned that it was difficult to envisage dying, because if there were an afterlife, she would be faced with having to meet both Stanley and my father. Jane had told me that she had been wrestling with the problem for some time. I said she didn't have to worry about James; he was surely used to meeting his lovers' husbands.

When I stood with my face at the glass of the French doors I saw that the flowers were yet to emerge in the pots on the terrace. What had appeared in eerie abundance were photographs of my father around the house. There was a new portrait of him on the bureau in the sitting room, in a suit and tie from the fresh-faced Oxford era, two more in Susie's office, both from the racy Californian period with the ocean at Malibu in the background, and another propped up on a bookshelf in her bedroom, from near a film set in Rome just before he died. I saw few photos of Stanley. I went to look at his ashes. Their receptacle was like a tube of pricey whisky.

THIRTY FIVE

The road to St Antonin

I HAD DONE SOME RESEARCH on death doulas, which I wanted to share with Susie. Death doulas are those people (mostly women) who act to help people out of life, rather than into it. I had come across an ambitious American lady called Christy Marek, who, I read in an interview, was 'certified by INELDA'. That's *The International End of Life Doula Association*. She had the certificate. I could see it on the wall in the photo. More, she had a website and a business: *Tending Life on The Threshold*. It looked profitable. That didn't feel entirely right to me.

Christy Marek said she wanted to 'improve the journey'. 'There is no medical role,' she continued, 'death doulas are companions and listeners. They attend.'

I showed Susie the article. She wasn't impressed.

'That's not what I need,' she said, shaking her head as she handed it back to me. 'I don't want a companion. I don't need one. No. Please. I want practical help.'

She was never going to respond well to having her hand held by someone cooing *Ahhh, bless* in her ear. Susie was a woman of action, not sentiment.

'What I want to know is how best to do it,' she said.

I could see that, and what Marek and INELDA were proposing was the equivalent of a mechanic who turned up when your car had broken down, brewed you a cup of tea, gave you lots of sympathy, and made no attempt to actually fix the engine.

One evening it grew warm enough to sit on the terrace. I hadn't been out there since the lunatic with the Prokofiev. Susie made her way towards the table, holding a glass of champagne, looked at the view, smiled, and lowered herself slowly into a chair.

'I've learnt you don't have to be at death's door to let go,' she said. 'I get ideas. Finally, I think. I have a big stash. But some are 150 mg slow-release and some are quick-release 50 mg. I go and put them in a blender. I don't know if the quick-release ones will have the same effect as the slow-release ones. I don't want to end up in Le Bon Saveur.'

'What's that?'

'It's the mental hospital in Gaillac where they put the failed suicides. The ones that didn't work out and are just, you know, in a coma, or worse.'

'There's a place just for them?' I asked.

'Them and others,' she said. I could see the thought worried her, but couldn't help smiling, it was such a ridiculous proposition.

'That's heavy,' I said.

'Some of my friends think what I am going to do is wrong and wicked. But they've not had the experience. Or were brought up in a religious atmosphere. Actually, Jesus didn't say anything about suicide. You have to stop being so scared of people. And scared of it.'

'That's true,' I said. 'That's what I hope the book is going to do.'

'Do you want to take notes?' she asked.

'Good idea,' I said. She waited for me to get a pen. When I returned she was getting into interview mode. The campaign was underway.

'Do you really think undignified, chronic pain is the only path out of life?' she asked an imaginary press conference while I scribbled on my pad. 'We have to have a mind shift. Break the taboo.' I could almost hear the camera shutters clicking. 'It's not doing anything for us, the way we die today.'

Neat quote, I thought. I could see she enjoyed having me as an attentive biographer. And I liked writing her portrait. She was a great subject. A better subject than mother. And this strange relationship, this playful and vicious tussle we were always engaged in, was the nearest we were going to get to being a standard-issue loving mother and son.

I passed her a magazine article about an invention called the Sarco, which the maker described as a suicide machine. *It enables its occupant* – it said – *to kill themselves at the press of a button.* You climbed into something that looked like a car roof box which then filled with nitrogen and gently suffocated you.

'It looks expensive,' she tutted. 'And anyway, how would we get it up the stairs? What about the paintwork?'

I thought that a comforting concern. There was life in her yet if she was worrying about the decor. I actually didn't want her to die. I was enjoying her company. Until she did the next thing, whatever that was.

'Actually, you can make it yourself with a 3D printer,' I said.

'I'm not relying on my printer.' she said.

'No,' I said. 'I know what you mean.'

'Anyway, I've decided how to do it.'

Oh yes, I thought. What game is this you are about to play with me? She had made one of her plans. Maybe I was the one playing the game, pretending she was not serious. How many times had she told me she was going to do this? I should have listened. This is what it meant: making a plan, and not being closeted about it. And living with it.

'OK,' I said. 'What are you going to do?'

'I am going to drive off a cliff.'

'Really?'

'Like Thelma and Louise.'

'Not in my car,' I said. Then I remembered my hatred of the hire car company in Toulouse. 'You could rent a car from Europcar and do it in that. They deserve it.'

'Can I have another glass of bubbly?' she asked.

As I poured she said, 'Drugs, even paraquat, can go wrong. I don't want to end like Madame Bovary.'

'Have you thought about *which* cliff?' I said. 'You know what the French are like with their health and safety. There are barriers everywhere.'

As I said the word barrier, I suddenly thought about my father's crash, and my mother's strange theory about his friend Basil's accident. Was she going for a tribute car wreck? To tie up her narrative neatly and give us all something to talk about?

'On the road to St Antonin,' she said.

'Really?' I said.

'Not the bottom road. The top road. It's steep and there's no barricade. And there's a long drop to the river. I know a good spot. I know *exactly* the spot.'

I had been up there once with my son, looking for a prehistoric cave. The single track road ran along the edge of a vertiginous drop. Deep in the gorge we had glimpsed the sparkle of the Tarn river.

The next day I took the car and drove on my own to survey the road to St Antonin. Under an armada of puffy white clouds holding disciplined formation, I passed through the oak, pine and juniper thicket of the Grésigne Forest, and out onto heathland. There were a few stone farmhouses on the plateau, some advertising honey for sale. The views were wide and empty. After ten minutes I spotted the streaked grey cliffs on the other side of the gorge. On my side, the ground fell away steeply. I parked the car and walked carefully to the edge of the slope, which was dotted with dry scrub and small Corsican pines, none of which would stop a car. Susie was right, it was a suitable place for a Thelma and Louise. And I didn't think God would impose a surcharge for an early return.

THIRTY SIX

Les flics

A WEEK PASSED AND I HAD to get back to Britain. On my last day I sat on the terrace and listened to Susie opine on the vexed issue of creating a foolproof watering operation for the new car park in the summer. Then she showed me the daisies, and explained how she was going to put them out in pots, reminiscing about her house in Gloucestershire where she had first grown daisy trees.

A few cars disturbed the gravel of her car park. She turned her head to see if they were berberis thieves, but they were tourists, in high spirits. The car doors slammed and we heard laughter. The village was coming to life. The season was renewing. Self-satisfied pigeons were cooing and fluttering under the eaves. The breeze possessed more than a hint of warmth and down in the valley the oak woods were quickening with unfurling leaves. Soon the girl with the piano would open her window, the holiday houses would awaken from their sleep, and the cloisters would fill with red-faced tourists.

If spring comes, can winter be far behind? I thought.

It was the order of these things. This was now how we were going to live. The drama of the end could be put aside without being removed. The matter was settled. Now all that had to be done was to do the living before the dying. But it had been decided and agreed: life was too sweet to waste with decrepitude.

Before I drove to the airport I decided to take a wander round the village. I ambled to Le Bar des Arcades, where I had spent so much time on my own over the past eighteen months. I wanted to bid George goodbye but he totally blanked me. I had developed a niggling fear. Now that we had spoken so openly about the end, it seemed as though the time between now and then would be too taken up with thinking about it. Which would be sad and grim, and in many ways counter to what Susie wanted to achieve by planning the drive to St Antonin. But I thought I had detected a sad atmosphere. I hoped Susie would still be able to smile again, and enjoy laughter.

When I got back Susie was at the railings on the terrace.

'There are some people here to see you,' she said.

'Who?'

'Two gendarmes. It's about a speeding ticket and something about insulting the Police. It's a serious offence in France. They have an arrest warrant. What have you done?' I thought immediately, this must be a wind-up, but I hadn't mentioned my speeding ticket letter to Susie.

'Shit,' I said.

'And that Italian woman Claudia's here.'

'What!!!' I dodged under the veranda.

'She's got someone called Gianni with her.'

'Gianni? What?' Gianni was the idiot who dropped his pants whenever he went into a restaurant. 'Tell them I've already have left for the airport. No ...' I thought of Claudia at customs control grabbling me, forcing me to take her out to lunch with Gianni and listen to her lecture me on the best place to buy sardines, while Gianni dropped his pants, before handing me over to the flics. 'Tell them I left yesterday.'

'I can't. The Police saw your passport on the table and have confiscated it. They know you're here. They are very nice actually. One used to be a pompier. I am thinking of opening a bottle of fizz. And Claudia is holding your hire-car keys very firmly in her fist. I don't think she's going to let them go till she sees you.'

'What!'

'You better come up.'

I trudged up the stairs. This was as nasty a pincer as I had ever felt closing in on me, and I had experienced a fair few.

'Bonjour! Bonjourno! Ciao!' I gaily called as I entered the room, where my mother stood, alone, with a broad smile on her face, holding a glass of sparkling wine.

'Allow me a titter,' she said.

I looked around. She was indeed on her own. 'How did you … Ah, of course, my book. *Our* book, I mean.'

'Your face was a sight,' she said.

'Gianni was a nice touch,' I said.

I laughed with her.

'You got me with him,' I said. 'The idiot.'

I gave her a hug, said goodbye and went downstairs to get my coat and bag. I took the house keys off my ring and hung them on the hooks by the door, next to Susie's car key. She would be needing that for the trip to St Antonin, whenever it was.

But right then, and I hoped for some time, it felt as though there was plenty of time to go, before it would be her time to go.